Get Paid
What You're
WORTH

Get Paid What You're WORTH

The Expert Negotiators' Guide to Salary and Compensation

ROBIN L. PINKLEY
AND
GREGORY B. NORTHCRAFT

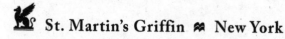 St. Martin's Griffin ✄ New York

Fifth Avenue, New York, NY 10010.

GET PAID WHAT YOU'RE WORTH. Copyright © 2000 by Robin L. Pinkley and Gregory B. Northcraft. All rights reserved. Printed in the United States of America. For information, address St. Martin's Press, 175 Fifth Avenue, New York, N.Y. 10010.

www.stmartins.com

Library of Congress Cataloging-in-Publication Data

Pinkley, Robin L.
    Get paid what you're worth : the expert negotiators' guide to salary and compensation / Robin L. Pinkley and Gregory B. Northcraft.
        p. cm.
    ISBN 0-312-24254-9 (hc)
    ISBN 0-312-30269-X (pbk)
    1. Wages. 2. Pay equity. 3. Negotiation in business.
4. Employment interviewing. I. Northcraft, Gregory B. II. Title.

HD4909.P54 2000
650.14—dc21   99-056770

10   9   8   7

This is dedicated to the ones we love.

To our parents, Pat and Bob Pinkley, and Julian and Sue Northcraft, for giving us the support and life skills to rise from our knees to stand.

To our long-term partners, Daniel Ness and Natasha, whose love and support gave us the confidence to walk forward.

And to Robin's beloved children, Erin and Kyle Ness, for teaching us the joy of running while howling at the moon.

CONTENTS

ACKNOWLEDGMENTS

We would like to acknowledge the many individuals who contributed to the successful completion of this project, including our many outstanding colleagues. Their support and ideas have been inspirational and instrumental, thus allowing us to leap forward in our thinking about these issues. In particular, we would like to thank John Andren, Max Bazerman, Becky Bennett, Rich Bettis, Jeanne Brett, Joan Brett, Jack Brittain, Susan Brodt, Donald Conlon, Len Greenhalgh, Terri Griffith, Al Hastorf, Rick Hoyle, Chet Insko, Ellen Jackofsky, Alfred Lindahl, Beta Mannix, Maggie Neale, Carolyn O'Reilly, John Slocum, Harris Sondak, John Thibaut, Don VandeWalle, and Kathy Williams.

We would also like to thank the executives and managers we have worked with at places like Allstate, AMRESCO, Andersen Consulting, ARCO, Blue Cross-Blue Shield, Ernst & Young, GE, Healthpoint, Heidrick & Struggles, Hewlett-Packard, I2, Mobil, Motorola, NASA, Reltec, SBC Communications, Smith-Kline-Beecham, Southwestern Bell, and Walt Disney World. We have learned more from these companies and the fine professionals who run them than we could ever teach them.

Of particular note are the hundreds of employers, employment professionals, and applicants who so generously contributed their time, knowledge, experience, concerns, and best practices, upon which this book is based. Lori Albert, Elizabeth Duncklee, Thomas Fernandez, Tom Fowler, Sara Hey, Laura Littlejohn, Steven Lubrana, Mike McMillin, Wesley Millican, Rick Miller, Barry Pryer, and Greg Satterwhite, who made up our panel of employment professionals, were particularly generous and forthcoming, as is evidenced by the quality of the advice they provide in Chapter 9.

Finally, we would like to thank those who have funded our research over the years, including: the Dispute Resolution Research Center at Northwestern University, the Ford Foundation, the Southern Methodist University Research Council, the Marilyn and Leo F. Corrigan Endowment, the Dorothy Cullum Faculty Fellowship, the John's Fellowship at the College of William and Mary, the University of Illinois, the National Science Foundation, and American Airlines.

Perhaps most of all, we thank the people who selflessly toiled behind the scenes, including Gayla Jackson and Lisa Shatz, both of whom invested significant time on the book while somehow finishing their MBA degrees at SMU; Melissa Barber, who spent a large portion of her summer retyping and editing the text; and Patrick O'Keefe, who helped us to add the finishing touches. All four provided valuable feedback and insight after reading the manuscript from a student/applicant perspective. We also appreciate the assistance of Camilla Drew and Grace Bowens, who kept the authors organized, and Jeanne Milazzo, who spent four long days and cancelled her Friday night plans to retype the manuscript from scratch and correct typo after typo after typo. We also appreciate Bob Gardner's willingness to incubate the project by putting us up and putting up with us in Colorado as we planned and outlined the book.

We are grateful to Steve Good and the other attorneys at Gardere & Wynne, L.L.P., for providing advice on legal issues, Barbara Estep for her many creative ideas regarding the marketing of the book, Vige Barrie and our publicist at St. Martin's press, Jenny Dworkin, for putting those ideas and their own marketing savvy into action. Finally, we are extremely grateful for the guidance, support, and enthusiasm of our agent, Jeremy Solomon, and our editor, Elizabeth Beier, both of whom wisely grasped the distinction between expertise in scholarship, consulting, and deal making from expertise in book writing.

PREFACE

You have probably purchased this book because you are negotiating a job offer or renegotiating a current contract. You are not alone. According to U.S. Department of Labor statistics, three-quarters of a million U.S. workers left their current jobs, over two million others reentered, and about a half million entered the U.S. workforce for the first time during one month in 1999. Some of these people are students acquiring their first job. Others have worked for many years but are seeking a change in position, company, industry, region, or country. Still others are forced into a new job search through downsizing or restructuring.

More than 50 percent of these people will accept their next job offer without the benefit of negotiation. Because they won't negotiate, most will receive lower salaries and fewer benefits than their employer was willing to pay. While those who do negotiate will fare better than those who do not, unless they negotiate effectively, they will receive less than they could. Nothing feels worse than beginning a new job only to discover that others less qualified than you receive better compensation. This is not how *you* want to begin your new job and this is not how *your employer* wants you to begin either.

People who receive less than they deserve, less than others in their position, or less than their employer is prepared to offer don't know how to negotiate effectively. **Many people think that they have to choose between a good deal and a good relationship. They don't know that you can negotiate while maintaining or even improving a relationship with a possible employer.** This book will prepare you to do just that.

The authors of this book have over thirty years of experience teaching people on both sides of the table how to negotiate successfully. In this book, we combine what we, our colleagues, and our clients have learned from years of consulting, teaching, research, and practice.

YOU WILL LEARN

- Which issues can be negotiated
- How to prepare for negotiation
- How to conduct a negotiation
- How to close the deal

You will benefit from:

Advice from the Experts. We combine what we have learned from years of training, consulting, and deal-making with the recommendations made by our expert panel of headhunters, recruiters, human resource professionals, and employers to give you strategies so state-of-the-art that you will find them in no other published book or article.

Advice from Those Who Have Been There. We include the experiences, stories, dilemmas, and questions shared by hundreds of job applicants who have struggled with the same issues you are struggling with now. We help you learn from their successes and avoid their failures.

Scientifically Proven Strategies. We go beyond what most negotiators *think* will work to tell you what we *know* will work. We provide strategies that have undergone rigorous scientific research and field testing by us or other researchers and scholars.

A Guide to Strategic Thinking. We teach you to avoid the biases and errors made by expert and novice negotiators alike that reduce the values obtained and harm the relationship.

A Guide to Specific Action. We teach you how to put your strategies into specific action. As a result, you won't have to guess what to do; you will know what to do, and how and when to do it.

Let's get started.

Get Paid
What You're
WORTH

1 IF YOU WANT IT, YOU'D BETTER NEGOTIATE FOR IT

Chris put down his *Wall Street Journal* and replaced it with *A Tale of Two Cities,* by Charles Dickens. He hoped reading an old favorite would distract him and help him relax a bit, although given the ache in his back, he wasn't hopeful.

"It was the best of times, it was the worse of times . . . " he read over and over.

"Yes, it is . . . ," he said aloud, as the issues he was trying to escape came back with a flood of emotion. The last two months had been an emotional and physical roller coaster. One moment he felt poised for success and the next as worthless as a 45 in a CD player. "How did I forget how time-consuming and stressful it is to be on the job market?" he wondered.

The last twenty-four hours had been stressful and exhausting. Last night he had forced himself to shove a burger down his throat as he searched the web for information to add to what he had learned from

1

Allied Products' annual report. He had gone to bed early only to toss and turn all night.

This morning had been a blur of coffee, burned toast, and a pretense of composure while he knotted his tie and made a mad dash to catch the train into the city.

"Get hold of yourself, man" he told himself. "They will be lucky to get me . . . they will be lucky to get me," he repeated to himself over and over like a mantra. "I have great credentials, three years of related work experience, a good salary history, an M.B.A. from a top business school, and a firm handshake. Just remember," he told himself as he walked in the front door of the skyscraper, "this interview thing is a two-way street."

Why You Must Negotiate

Job applicants negotiate because they want to walk away with more than they are initially offered. They want the final deal to include everything the company is willing and able to give them. We wrote this book to provide you with a foundation for understanding how to claim more of what's at stake in *your* negotiations.

Imagine that an employer has $100,000 left in the budget for a number of things, including hiring a new employee. Employers know that the less they spend on a new employee, the more they will have left to spend on other things or the better their profit figures will look for the year. Thus, employers negotiate with job applicants to try to keep as much of that $100,000 in reserve as possible. Of course, job applicants want to do as well as possible for themselves. If they knew there was $100,000 available, they would want to get as much of it as possible. Both employers and applicants want to claim as much as they can of the $100,000 at stake. But claiming value requires that we exchange value.

When you accept a job offer, you exchange your education, experience, expertise, and effort for the salary, benefits, opportunity, and even friendships associated with the job. Ultimately each party in the negotiation must decide how much value he/she must claim to justify the exchange.

Job applicants who negotiate what they will get in exchange for the work that they do receive salaries and benefits of significantly greater value than candidates who do not. While most employers prefer that you show up on the first day happy and committed instead of disappointed and disillusioned, few will compensate you more than they need to. In fact, employers routinely will offer you less than they ultimately expect to compensate you with the expectation that you will negotiate. Of the employers we surveyed, 100 percent told us that it is acceptable for job applicants to attempt to negotiate a job offer. Of these employers 90 percent told us that their initial offer was less that they were willing to pay because they expected the applicant to negotiate. For example, when we told employers that their top applicant would

- *Reject* an offer of $35,000
- Accept an offer of $38,000, with *dissatisfaction*
- Accept an offer of $41,000, with *satisfaction*
- Accept an offer of $44,000, with *pleasure*
- Accept an offer of $48,000, with *great pleasure,*

50 percent said that they would offer the applicant an amount that would lead the applicant to accept and be satisfied (a salary

of $41,000); 40 percent said they would offer the amount that would lead the applicant to accept and be happy ($44,000); and another 10 percent said they would offer only the amount required to produce an acceptance, even though the applicant would be dissatisfied ($38,000). In each case, they told us that they would ultimately pay more to get this applicant if the applicant negotiated, but that they would be delighted to get the applicant for less. **Bottom line: If you want something, you had better negotiate for it.**

One study found that men who negotiate receive 4.3 percent higher salaries than men who do not, while women who negotiate receive on average 2.7 percent higher salaries than women who do not. Despite the fact that few of the applicants in that study had received training in effective negotiation, those who negotiated were more successful than those who did not.

Though it is unclear why the women in the study benefited less from negotiation than did the men, many recruiters tell us that women use less assertive tactics than do men. In this book, we will explain how to use tactics that are *tough* when it comes to the issues, but *gentle* when it comes to the people involved.

A Lifetime of Benefits

The compensation package you obtain today affects your life today and tomorrow. As you may know, applicants with work experience are almost always asked for their salary history. Employers request the information for two reasons: (1) to determine how much they need to pay you, and (2) to see how you compare to others in the same market.

Applicants with identical experience and performance records but different salary histories are rated differently by employers. If your compensation record is better than others, employers will assume that your performance record is better too. **Salary history sends a signal that profoundly effects performance reviews, raises, and job offers—for years to come.** Make it a goal to enter an organization or job market making no less than other applicants. Accepting less will imply that you have less value than other new hires.

Even we were surprised when we calculated the total cost of not negotiating over a man's or woman's career. Assuming (1) a base salary of $50,000, (2) a mean annual pay increase of 3–4 percent, (3) a change in job every eight years (conservative given that most people change jobs more often on average), (4) a fifty-year career, and for comparison, including the 4.3 percent salary boost traditionally obtained by men who negotiate, and the 2.7 percent salary boost traditionally obtained by women who negotiate, we found astonishing benefits for those who negotiated over those who did not.

THE BENEFITS OF NEGOTIATING

- Men who negotiate will receive $1,714,779 *more* in the course of their careers than those who do not.

- Women who negotiate will receive $1,040,917 *more* in the course of their careers than those who do not.

If you don't negotiate, you might (1) accept a good job that could have been a great job if you had negotiated or (2) turn down a poor job that could have been a good job if you had ne-gotiated. Without negotiation, your choice will be based on in-complete information. The only thing harder than comparing apples to oranges is comparing half an apple to an orange. Yet this is exactly what you do when you fail to negotiate an offer. Avoid this trap! Claim the best available job with the most value—through effective negotioation.

Why Applicants Don't Negotiate

Only 50 percent of the applicants we surveyed said that they had negotiated their last job offer. Recruiters told us that in re-ality only about 25 percent of applicants negotiate. After doing everything in their power to land the job, many applicants make one of two postoffer mistakes:

COMMON POSTOFFER MISTAKES

- Gratefully accepting the offer without negotiating
- Negotiating without considering other options or gen-erating alternatives

---

It may seem easy to simply say yes, but this strategy is short-sighted and costly. So why don't more applicants negotiate the offer once they have received it? We think the answer has to do with fear.

JOB APPLICANTS' MOST COMMON FEARS ABOUT NEGOTIATION

- Fear of the employer's perception
- Fear of losing the offer
- Fear of conflict
- Fear of the employer's superior power
- Fear of emotion
- Fear of negotiating poorly

Fear of the Employer's Perception. Applicants often fear that negotiating will make them appear cheap, selfish, cocky, ungrateful, or (shudder!) more concerned about what the employer has to offer them than about what they can offer the employer. We asked corporate headhunters and placement officers which of the following job applicants they would find the most impressive:

WHO IS THE MOST IMPRESSIVE?

- The applicant who accepts an offer as made
- The applicant who negotiates the offer in a professional, problem-solving manner
- The applicant who negotiates the offer in a demanding manner

Eighty percent told us that the job applicant who negotiates in a professional manner would make the best impression. Only 20 percent said they would be most impressed by the applicant who accepted the offer as made. Applicants are perceived more favorably if they negotiate well than if they do not negotiate.

Fear of Losing the Offer. Job applicants tell us that they are afraid they could lose the offer if they don't accept it as it is. We asked employers if they had ever revoked an offer, and if so, why? Only 30 percent of the recruiters, headhunters, and placement officers we surveyed had *ever* seen an offer revoked. In no case was an offer revoked because the applicant had negotiated. Instead, offers were revoked because an applicant had misrepresented his or her qualifications or because the applicant dragged the negotiation out so long that the circumstances changed and the position was no longer needed. **Offers are not revoked because a job applicant negotiates but because of how the applicant negotiates.**

Fear of Conflict. For many job applicants negotiation implies conflict. They assume that the only way they can win more in a negotiation is by making the other side lose something. But this doesn't need to be the case. As you'll see in chapter 4, **effective negotiators know how to find enough value for all parties in a negotiation.**

Let's say you and a friend decide to go to a movie but you disagree about which movie to see. You've got three choices: (1) You can debate for hours and miss the movie (a poor solution because no one is happy); (2) one of you can choose the movie this week and the other next week (an acceptable solution but one that requires that each of you see a movie you are not interested in); or (3) you can each explain "why" you made your selection and look for an alternative that fulfills both of your underlying interests. If you selected your movie because you are in the mood for a comedy and your friend selected his/her movie because of the director, this discussion could allow you to select a third choice: A comedy directed by the preferred director would allow you both to get what you want. This example illustrates that **effective negotiators can be firmly committed to getting what they want but still allow the other side to get what they want too. The other side doesn't have to lose in negotiation in order for you to win.**

Fear of the Employer's Superior Power. More often than not, applicants feel that employers have all the power in contract negotiations. This is a misperception. Getting an initial offer from an employer means that you are their preferred applicant. The negotiation begins when you have been asked to join their company but you have not yet accepted. You might be surprised to find out that **employers often believe that it is the applicant who has more power!** In fact, recruiters tell us that they feel downright powerless when their preferred applicants have competing offers. We will talk more about power, the role it plays, and how to create it in chapter 6. In the meantime, it takes two to negotiate. Remember that no one can force you to accept an offer. Ultimately you have control over what you accept and what you reject. And *that's* power.

Fear of Emotion. Many people fear that the negotiation will get emotional and as a result too personal. Negotiation does not have to be personal. **Conflict is a less likely product of negotiation if you remember to make the negotiation about the issues—not about the people.** Fear of emotion leads to inaction and the tendency to settle prematurely. Inaction means both lost value and a lost opportunity to make a positive impression.

Fear of Negotiating Poorly. This is the only fear that seems justified to us. The desire to negotiate well is not sufficient. You need to know *how* to negotiate well. Fortunately, the doctors are "in" and we have the cure. The cure is this book, so read on.

- Negotiation determines how much an employer is prepared to give you and how much you obtain. Only by negotiating can you know which job is really the best job for you.

- Applicants who negotiate their job offers receive salaries and benefits of significantly more value. This becomes very important over the "life of the employee."

- The compensation package you obtain today affects your life today—and also your future job offers. When you get a job offer, you *must* negotiate.

2 BEFORE YOU RECEIVE AN OFFER: BUILDING A FOUNDATION FOR SUCCESS

Sara had tried not to corner Chris the minute she got home from work. She was itching to find out about his interview, but didn't want to push him in case it had not gone well. Finally she could contain herself no longer.

"So how did it go?" she blurted out.

"Wow, you lasted twelve full minutes before you cornered me. That could be a record," Chris said with a smile. "I think it went pretty well, all things considering," he added.

"Considering what?" she asked with concern, as she moved to give him a protective hug.

"Well, considering they ended the day by pairing me with four other candidates who all want the same job. They herded us into a room, told us to act like a team, gave us a problem to solve, and then reminded us that only two of us would receive an offer. Can you believe it?" he asked. "They told us to act like a team, only to remind us that we were in competition with one another. It makes you wonder, doesn't it?"

"Wonder what?" Sara asked.

"Oh, I don't know, lots of things. Like what they were looking for and whether the task they gave us was a test or just an indication of the kind of mixed messages I will get if I get the offer and go to work for them," Chris said reflectively.

"Good question," Sara said. "I guess it could be either. So what did you do?"

"Well, I decided to just be myself. I put aside my concerns and just focused on the problem and working with my teammates. In fact, we worked well together. I really liked all four candidates. At least this company has a good eye for talent," Chris admitted.

"So what happens now?" Sara asked.

"They said they would make a decision in thirty days. I guess I will just have to wait until then and focus on the challenges in my current job. There is not much else I can do . . . but wait," Chris said with a shrug.

Successful negotiation begins long before you discuss an offer with a recruiter.

Before your first discussion with the employer, you should already know what you want to discuss, where you want the discussion to go, and how you might get it there. You should even know what the employer might want the discussion to include, and where the recruiter might want the discussion to go. The more you know *before* you start talking to the employer, the more likely your negotiation will be successful.

Avoid Premature Job Selection

It can prove costly to decide prematurely which company to work for. Yet some job applicants do; in fact, some applicants decide before they get their first interview. They make their decision based on information about the company's reputation, market performance, size, and location. In reality, there are many more factors you need to consider before you zero in on a preferred employer.

FACTORS THAT SHOULD INFLUENCE YOUR JOB CHOICE

- Status and reputation of the employer
- Nature of the position
- Opportunities for the future
- Culture and organizational environment
- People you will work with and for
- Salary and compensation package

While the first two factors do not require an interview to determine, the third, fourth, and fifth do. The last factor (salary and compensation) will be uncertain until you receive and negotiate an offer. The employers we surveyed told us that their first offer (salary and compensation) is rarely their *best offer*. They keep some value "in reserve" because they expect you to negotiate. The negotiation process will help you uncover how much the company is prepared to give you and determine how much you get for yourself. **Only by negotiating can you determine which company is best for you.**

Ultimately the most valuable job offer you receive may not be from your first-choice company. Sure, you would be smart to accept an offer from your first-choice company if no other company could top their offer. But your preferred company may not offer the best compensation package because they can probably attract strong applicants without doing so. They can compete in other nontangible ways. In the end, you may need to decide just how much you are willing to give up to work for your first-choice company. **The best job for you is the one that offers you the most *total* value**—value you get from the compensation package *plus* all other important factors.

In preparation for your meeting with prospective employers you'll need a framework to help you organize and make sense of the information you've obtained about each relevant factor. As soon as you find out who you will be interviewing with, you should start to gather information. Do you or your friends have contacts in the organization? Do you know anyone who interviewed with them last year? Did they get an offer? What was in the offer? Talk to friends, check on the Internet, read whatever you can find in the library, and ask your local job placement office to answer the questions you have about each factor.

The more you can find out about a company *before* the interview, the less dependent you are on the interview process for understanding how much value the company can offer you. Employers are often surprised at how little applicants know about their company. Of course, this puts applicants at a tremendous disadvantage, since **information is power.** You need to know as much as you can about the value any company might offer you and the value that you can offer the company in return.

Of course, the amount of value that others have received from any given company is not necessarily what you should expect to receive. Remember, the value the company is prepared to offer is only important if you get them to offer it. It takes negotiation to determine how much value you can obtain. Your goal is to do a better job negotiating the offer than previous applicants and gain more of the available value for yourself.

Avoid Premature Negotiation

Employers often ask what salary or compensation you are looking for before making you an offer. If you are asked this question, first respond with a statement that acknowledges the importance of this topic but defers it until after the offer is made. For example, you might say:

"I realize that salary is an important issue, and I hope to discuss it with you in the near future. But I'd prefer that we first determine how I'd fit within your organization on other issues such as education, experience, and expertise."

Avoid a discussion of salary and compensation if you can until you have the employer convinced that they really want— no, *need*—to hire you. Besides avoiding a debate, deferring this discussion keeps you from losing the job because you inadvertently ask for more than they want to pay. It also keeps you from asking for too little in order to keep your name in the pool of potential hires. You want to sell before you trade.

Build Your Side of the Playing Field

Use the information you gather to build your side of the negotiation playing field.

YOUR SIDE OF THE PLAYING FIELD INCLUDES

- The specific *issues* you wish to negotiate

- The *issue range* for each issue: includes all of the settlement options for that issue ranging from the least acceptable or *bottom line* to the most desired or *target*

- The *issue weight* for each issue and each issue option: the value or importance of each issue option relative to all other options

- The *interests* that underlie the issues

- The *package range:* includes your bottom line and target for the overall deal

- Information about your *best alternative* offer

Create a Preference Sheet

Organize this information into a diagram that details your preferences so that you can compare and contrast the value of the offers you receive. We call this diagram a preference sheet. Chris's preference sheet is displayed in table 2.1

19

TABLE 2.1: CHRIS'S PREFERENCE SHEET

Attractiveness of the Opportunity	Weight	This Offer	Alternative Offer
■ Exceptional	9,000		
■ Very Good	6,000		6,000
■ Good	3,000		
■ Adequate [Bottom line]	0		
Salary			
■ $60,000	6,000		
■ $55,000	4,000		
■ $50,000	2,000		2,000
■ $45,000 [Bottom line]	0		
Moving-Expense Coverage			
■ 100 percent	3,000		3,000
■ 75 percent	2,000		
■ 50 percent	1,000		
■ 0 percent [No bottom line]	0		
Signing Bonus			
■ 10–15 percent	3,000		
■ 6–9 percent	2,000		2,000
■ 1–5 percent	1,000		
■ 0 percent [No bottom line]	0		
Starting Date			
■ June 1	1,500		
■ July 1	1,000		
■ August 1	500		500
■ September 1 [Bottom line]	0		
Vacation Time—Year 1			
■ 4 weeks	750		
■ 3 weeks	500		
■ 2 weeks	250		250
■ 1 week [Bottom line]	0		
Package Target			
	22,250=target		13,750=bottom line

Let's walk through Chris' preference sheet to examine each component used to describe and build his part of the playing field.

ISSUES

Issues are *what* we negotiate and consist of whatever is at stake for either side in the discussion. In a negotiation like the one Chris is facing with Mr. Burton, salary is an issue. In fact, salary tends to be the issue that is foremost in the minds of both candidates and recruiters. While salary is always crucial, negotiations include many other issues of value and importance. Sit down and consider all of the issues of relevance to you before you attempt to negotiate. These issues include tangibles, such as vacation time, car allowance, and moving expenses, as well as intangibles like the status and growth potential of the company, how interesting or enjoyable the work is likely to be, or the promotion potential for upward mobility.

Chris decided that six issues were important to him, including the attractiveness of the opportunity, salary, moving-expense coverage, signing bonus, starting date, and vacation time.

What follows is a list of the issues most commonly discussed when negotiating a job contract. Issues listed first are common for all titles and levels of seniority. Issues at the end of the list are more difficult to obtain and are generally associated with very senior, high-status positions. Generally, you can expect salary to represent a smaller and smaller portion of your total compensation as your position becomes more senior. Corporate officers may receive as little as 10 percent or 20 percent of their total compensation in salary, with the remainder coming from bonuses or equity.

NEGOTIABLE ISSUES

Basic Compensation

- Salary
- Salary increases
- Start date
- Sales commission
- Vacation time/holidays
- Work schedule or hours

Additional Compensation

- Bonus structure
- Signing bonus
- Promotion schedule
- Larger salary at specific time
- Title/wage grade
- Profit sharing
- Equity benefits

Stock Options: This gives the employee the right to purchase a certain number of shares at a fixed price. The employee has no risk and is able to receive the value of the appreciation of the stock.

Restricted Stock: This stock is usually issued at no cost in the exchange for services provided by the employee.

Additional Equity Benefits: Stock Appreciation Rights, Phantom Stock, Equity Packages, Stock Purchase Requirements.

Insurance Coverage

- General coverage
- Medical insurance (may include spouse and children)
- Life insurance
- Dental insurance
- Optical insurance (glasses/contacts)

- Accidental death insurance
- Disability insurance
- Business travel insurance

Retirement Benefits

- 401k—waive eligibility period
- Pension
- Guaranteed age of retirement

Relocation Assistance

- Green card
- Select geographic location
- Spouse placement
- Time spent traveling
- Moving expenses (furniture, shipping of cars, boats, pets, etc.)
- Difference in mortgage rates
- Travel costs when looking at new homes
- Salary adjustments to meet needs of new location

Additional Perks

- Personal

    Child care

    Company car

    Vehicle allowance

    Parking reimbursement

    Phone allowance for cellular phone

    Health club membership

    Golf club membership

- Job specific

    Travel budget

Specific job functions

Secretarial support

Expectation of workload

Ability to select a team

Flexible work schedule

Termination clauses

Performance measurements

Start-up funding for projects

Laptop computer and other technology

Tuition reimbursement

Office—size and location

Contract with layoff provision

Title upon graduation

Overtime/travel compensation

■ Career advancement

Management development programs

Training/education

Access to technology (home equipment usage)

Access to strategic plan activity

Good negotiators determine what issues are important to them, including: what issues they think are going to be negotiated, what issues they *want* to negotiate, and even what issues they may *not* want to negotiate. Raising an issue tells the other side that it is something you want or need to discuss. Not discussing an issue is the same as agreeing to the other side's position on it. If you do not discuss moving expenses, it is the same as agreeing to no moving expenses! Be ready to raise all of the issues that are relevant to you. Begin by listing all of the tangible and intangible issues that can distinguish one job offer from another.

ISSUE CHARACTERISTICS

Every issue has two characteristics that determine how it can and should be negotiated. The first characteristic is the **issue range,** and the second is the **issue weight.**

Issue Range. At the bottom of the range is the least acceptable option (called a **bottom line**) and at the top of the range is the most attractive option (called a **target**). For example, if $45,000 is the lowest salary Chris will accept and he hopes to obtain $60,000, then his salary range is $45,000–$60,000.

Bottom Line. Carefully consider the bottom line or least acceptable option for each issue. Don't select a bottom line unless you would reject an offer that does not match or exceed it. Inexperienced negotiators often allow trivial issues to become deal breakers because they picked a poor bottom line. The bottom line for each issue should reflect how much it would take to make a deal acceptable to you. For example, Chris selected $45,000 as his bottom line for salary because that figure will allow him to pay his bills, support his family, and go to work with his head held high.

You should not select a bottom line for an issue that you are willing to give up. For example, Chris did not pick a bottom

25

line for moving-expense coverage or signing bonus because neither is a deal breaker for him. Even though he would like a high level of each, he will not reject a valuable offer just because it includes neither.

Target. At the top end of the range is your target or your best hope for that issue. Targets are derived from information like the "top" of the market (the best offers you've heard about). A target gives you a goal to shoot for. We find that applicants who focus on the bottom line tend to accept offers just above that bottom line. In contrast, negotiators who commit to the bottom line (are unwilling to accept offers that provide less value) but focus on the target, walk away with offers of significantly higher value.

Targets not only push you to obtain value above your bottom line but also help improve the employer's perception of your worth. Let's say, for example, that the market salary for the job ranges from $40,000 to $60,000. You can strategically convey your target of $60,000 to the recruiter by saying something like:

"I think my experience and education put me at the top of the market, which is around $60,000. That is the figure I am shooting for. Do you agree?"

This discussion strategically shifts the employer away from less strategic figures like the amount you are currently making, the amount he/she just offered you, or the market average. It's better to let the employer move you down from your target than to try to move him/her up from the initial offer.

Information about what range to expect in your job market can be obtained through a number of sources. Listed below are a number of available resources.

Helpful Sources for Salary Comparison

PUBLISHED SOURCES (AVAILABLE AT THE PUBLIC LIBRARY OR BOOKSTORE)

- *Occupational Outlook Handbook* and *America's Top 300 Jobs*
  These two sources provide information on both starting and average pay ranges across a variety of industries. Updated by the U.S. Department of Labor every two years, these books provide information on occupations ranging from government positions to technology. The information provided is important in helping the job applicant know what to expect at all experience levels.

- *The Career Connection for College Education: A Guide to College Majors and Related Career Opportunities* and the *Career Connection for Technical Education: A Guide to Technical Training and Related Career Opportunities*
  Fred Rowe's books provide an easy way to apply one's course of study to possible career choices. Within the books are details concerning average salary earnings, including the starting point of most careers. Finally, Rowe correlates the effect of continuing education on your salary within the career you have selected.

- *Guide to America's Federal Jobs*
  Interested in a job with the federal government? If so, then this is a book you need to get. The book details all positions available, college training needed, and pay ranges for all divisions of the federal government. Also included are additional details about various kinds of compensation and perks one receives while working for the government.

- *White Collar Pay: Private Goods–Producing Industries*
  Produced by the U.S. Bureau of Labor Statistics, this book provides an excellent source for information on white-collar jobs in the manufacturing industry. Details on average salary and compensation are also provided.

- *The American Almanac of Jobs and Salaries (Avon Books, N.Y.)*
  This book provides the wages for specific occupations, as well as job groups across a variety of industries. Also provided are trends in employment and wages.

SALARY COMPARISON ACROSS GEOGRAPHIC REGIONS

- *Career Guide to America's Top Industries*
  This source tracks over sixty major industries across various geographic regions. A detailed description of each industry's employment, projections for the future, working conditions, typical occupations, training needed, average salary, and advancement opportunities are also provided. Also included is a comparison of industries. This reveals the earning differences across regions for the same kind of work.

■ *State & Metropolitan Area Data Book*
Published by the U.S. Department of Commerce, this
book provides statistical data from both public and private
agencies. Information is also provided on employment
growth rates, unemployment rates, and the population
growth for every state. Furthermore, the average income is
listed for metropolitan areas across the country.

■ *AMS Office, Professional & Data Processing Salaries Report
(Administrative Management Society Office, Washington, D.C.)*
This is an excellent resource, useful in understanding how
jobs and salaries differ across geographic regions. The sur-
vey contains information on thousands of jobs. Specific
information is given on salaries and wage rates, cost of
living for different areas, number of people involved in oc-
cupation, and projected changes within the industry. Furthermore, the information is divided geographically. This
source would be a wonderful aid in deciding where to lo-
cate.

INTERNET SOURCES

■ Job Star
This site provides salary information, personal surveys
about self-knowledge, and negotiation strategies for achiev-
ing your optimum salary. The sites' information is derived
from local newspapers, general periodicals, as well as trade
and professional journals.
Web Site Address: http://www.townonline.com/working/

- PinPoint Salary Service
  This site can be accessed via the Internet or, for personal service, by telephone. The group will research your job and provide you with information on a pay comparison analysis with other individuals in your region.
  Web Site Address: http://members.aol.com/payraises
  Phone Number: (773) 4–SALARY or (773) 472–5279

- Homefair
  This web site provides information on the actual cost of living in a particular city. The site uses a tool called the "salary calculator" that evaluates the city you have selected, a salary you are earning, and your current base location. The output gives you a comparable salary in your new location.
  Web Site Address: http://www.homefair.com/homefair/cmr/salcalc.html

OTHER USEFUL SALARY COMPARISON SOURCES

- Professional Associations
  Most occupations have some sort of professional association at both a local and national level. The associations provide their members with salary surveys, as well as information on trends, pay rates, and job leads. Furthermore, it is an excellent tool for networking.

- Chamber(s) of Commerce
  Look to the Economic Development Division of the Chamber of Commerce to see salary and wage rate trends within the region. This is also an excellent way to network.

- Local Government Assistance Programs
  Often there are small-business associations that will be able to provide information on salaries across industries for small businesses. This is an excellent way to get the specific job facts you need about your chosen industry.

- Local/Area Business Organizations
  Organizations, such as "The Association for Women in Communications," offer an opportunity not only to create a network but also to attain salary information about various industries.

ISSUE WEIGHT

The importance of an issue can be based on objective criteria like dollar value or on very subjective criteria like *intrinsic* value—how you feel about the issue. Issue importance is a very personal decision. Your underlying interests should determine the relative importance of each issue and the order you put them in.

Assigning a weight is not difficult. In fact, you can create any point system you like. Assign points to issues and the options for each issue in a way that reflects the relative importance of each to you.

If you look at Chris's preference sheet (table 2.1), you will see that he is most concerned about the attractiveness of the opportunity (0–9000 points) and least concerned about vacation time (0–750 points). Moving-expense coverage (0–3,000 points) and signing bonus (0–3,000 points) are of equal importance to him.

This information will help Chris compare the value of his alternative offer (total point value—13,750) to the offer made by the company he is talking to now, when and if he gets it (some value between 0 and 22,250). It will also help him determine his priorities and what trade-offs to accept. For example, Chris would rather accept an offer that includes an exceptional opportunity (9,000 points) and a salary of $55,000 (4,000 points) than an offer that provides a very good opportunity (6,000 points) and a higher salary of $60,000 (6,000 points). Everything else being equal, the first offer will provide him more total value (13,000 points versus 12,000 points) than the second.

Underlying Interests

An underlying interest is the *why* behind the *what* you are negotiating. *What* Chris wants is a high salary. More important than what he wants, however, is *why* he wants it. He may want a high salary because of the nice lifestyle it would provide or because of the status it would give him with his peers. If Chris focuses on *what* he wants instead of *why* he wants it, he may accept the salary he wants only to lose the lifestyle he was really after. For example, an applicant who does not realize that lifestyle goals underlie his objective of obtaining a high salary may turn down an offer of $60,000 in Atlanta for a $70,000 offer in New York, although the first would have given him a better lifestyle. In this case, it is not really salary (an issue) that is important. It is what Chris can obtain through salary that is important (his underlying interests). While more salary will certainly mean more benefit or value, Chris needs to remember that there may be other, better ways to obtain that benefit or value than salary. Part of negotiation is to discover and create alternative ways to find value.

You must be as clear about the underlying interests you desire as you are about the issues you negotiate. You need to be absolutely clear about "why" this particular package of issues is important and how obtaining it will meet your interests. The better you understand your underlying interests, the better your ability to find opportunities during the negotiation to fulfill them.

PACKAGE RANGE

Just as you identified a bottom line and target for your issues, you should pick a bottom line and target for the entire agreement. These figures should reflect the least amount of total value you would be willing to accept before calling it quits and rejecting the offer and the overall value you are targeting. Your package's target should be based on the total point value you would receive if an offer included everything you wanted for each issue in the negotiation. For Chris, his agreement target is 22,250 points. Your package's bottom line should be based on the total point value you *must have* before you decline the offer. As soon as you obtain an offer that exceeds your bottom line, you should raise your bottom line to reflect the value of that offer. Since Chris has an offer from another company worth 13,750 points, this is his package bottom line.

When you compare one offer to another always compare the *overall* value of each. Applicants have a tendency to give undo weight to salary or job assignment and to allow these issues to dominate their decision. Our point system will help you incorporate your concerns about salary without forgetting about all of the other issues in the offer—and how those other issues can provide you the value you may not be able to get from salary.

Use the following steps to create your preference sheet:

HOW TO CREATE A PREFERENCE SHEET

- List all of the *issues* you want included in the package.

- Determine the *issue range* (bottom line and target) for each issue.

- Determine the relative importance of each issue and assign each an *issue weight*.

- Determine the overall value of your *best alternative* offer.

- Determine your agreement *package range*.

Order Your Interviews

An important point to consider during your preparations is the **order of your interviews.** The order in which you arrange your interviews can have a profound effect on the job you ultimately accept and the offer associated with that job.

Just as you are anxious to get the job you want most, employers are anxious to hire their top candidates. Because of this, employers may pressure candidates into a quick response by giving them "exploding offers." Exploding offers are offers that are revoked if not accepted by a specified date. **Ordering interviews helps you avoid exploding offers.**

You should schedule your best prospects or high-priority companies early. Doing so will make it less likely than an "exploding offer" will be a problem. If you interview with your high-priority companies first—the companies that will *probably* offer you the most value—an exploding offer is only likely to force you to take the offer you may have wanted anyway. (We will provide detailed solutions for responding to exploding offers in chapter 6).

The critical exception to this "most-promising-interviews-early" rule is your first interview. **Your very first interview should be treated as a practice session,** and therefore your very first interview should be with an organization of low initial priority. This will allow you to experiment and practice your interview technique at minimal cost. The tactics and strategies we describe in this book all work better with practice. The more familiar you are with what you may be asked, or even how it may be asked, the easier it will be for you to handle it effectively and successfully. That is, the easier it will be to obtain *all* the value you can in your offers.

- The more you find out about a company *before* the interview, the less you have to depend on the interview to tell you how much value a company can offer you.

- **Issues** are "what" we negotiate, and **underlying interests**—the value those issues offer us—are "why" we negotiate. When you negotiate issues, you are really negotiating for the value those issues give you.

- A **preference sheet** allows you to compare and contrast the value associated with each issue, and with each offer, and what is most important to you.

- Schedule your most promising prospects early, right after a practice session with your least promising organization.

3 GETTING THE OFFER: FIRST STEPS

Chris looked around the office nervously. Golf trophies, a model sail-boat, a duck decoy—Mr. Burton was obviously the outdoors type.

"So, Chris," Mr. Burton began, "I know you're probably a bit anxious so let me cut to the chase and let you know that we have decided to make you an offer. Congratulations."

Chris managed a grateful smile as he shook Mr. Burton's hand. Anxious, Chris thought, is quite an understatement. "Thank you, Mr. Burton," he said. "I am delighted. This is a truly great opportunity for me. How do you think we should proceed?"

Mr. Burton continued. "Let's see if we can get this thing signed, sealed, and delivered right away. Just to put your mind at ease, I want you to know that we don't usually negotiate salary. We've determined what an appropriate salary would be—based on a lot more information than you have. I'm sure you'll be pleased." He slid a piece of paper over to Chris.

Chris's hand shook a bit as he glanced quickly at the piece of paper. The salary was fine, but nothing special. In fact, it was very close to where Sara predicted they would start. Chris decided to jump right in. "What about other issues, Mr. Burton? You know, like a signing bonus."

"Well, we don't normally offer a signing bonus. As for the rest of the package someone from Human Resources will go over all of that with you. I'm sure it will be fine. So if you'll just initial that letter and write in your social security number, I'll get your paperwork started."

Chris swallowed. This seemed to be happening way too fast. "What about the starting date?"

"Well," offered Mr. Burton, "that depends on what openings are still available. I have you slotted in to start in two months, in Operations at the Charlotte office."

Charlotte sounded great. But Operations? Wasn't Marketing supposed to be the "fast-track" in this company? "Well, what if I don't want to work in Operations?" Inwardly, Chris grimaced. He realized that had sounded a bit too aggressive.

Mr. Burton paused. "You mean you don't want the job?"

First Steps

Being a good negotiator means being able to effectively manage the give-and-take of the negotiation exchange so that you can claim what you want and have the other side agree to it. **You don't obtain any value in a negotiation until the other side says, "Yes!"**

We will address two "first steps" in managing the negotiation process:

**FIRST STEPS FOR
GETTING THE BALL ROLLING**

- Enlist their help.
- Manage the flow of information.

Enlisting Their Help

The old adage, "You only get one chance to make a first impression," is critical in a job negotiation. In fact, that one chance is often very brief, perhaps as little as a few minutes. Whether your negotiation is over the phone or face-to-face, the first things you do and the first things you say determine whether anything else you do will be successful. So how should you start?

The answer to this question goes back to the definition of negotiation. **Negotiation is the process through which two or more people decide what each will get in an exchange.** Negotiation is a joint process. We can only claim the value we want if the other side agrees. Therefore, the first goal of any job negotiation should be to enlist the assistance of the employer. You want to form a partnership with them and to get them working with you to solve the problem, "How can we come to a mutually satisfactory agreement?" There are four steps to enlisting their help:

HOW TO ENLIST THE EMPLOYER'S HELP

- Break the ice.

- Create a professional investment.

- Find a personal connection.

- Be sincere and credible.

BREAKING THE ICE

The process of negotiation involves a great deal of uncertainty. And when there is uncertainty, there will also be anxiety: anxiety about a "tug-of-war," anxiety about appearing foolish, even anxiety about not knowing what is right. Anxiety is stressful. Anxiety makes people rigid, and anxiety makes people defensive. **The best first step in any negotiation is to break the ice by reducing the other side's anxiety.**

If you've reached the point where they are talking about compensation, somebody (and probably several somebodies) has already invested effort in you as an applicant. And they've invested that effort without getting anything concrete in return. **You can make the other side less defensive and less anxious by giving them something right now in return for their investment.** This something is your thanks for being considered. It doesn't cost you anything and they'll appreciate it. It may seem trite, but people like to be thanked for what they have done. Thanking the employer sets a very positive tone for the remainder of the discussion. It also models good exchange behavior—behavior that you will want to engage in later when you discuss the issues and options that provide value.

CREATING PROFESSIONAL INVESTMENT

In the heat of a compensation negotiation, it is easy to view the exchange as being about give-and-take on the *issues*—such as exchanging less salary for more moving expenses or exchanging more health care for less life insurance. It is easy to lose sight of the fact that **the real exchange is the exchange between what you bring to the job, and what the company gives you in return.** The more they think you are worth, the more they will be willing to compensate you.

The best way to form a problem-solving partnership with the other side is to remind them of the value you bring. In particular, highlight the *unique* value that you bring to the job—whatever you have that they cannot "buy" elsewhere. Maybe it's your experience, and maybe it's your effort. Whatever it is, **focus on the unique value you bring at the beginning of the negotiation to get the employer invested in hiring you.** You want them to decide that they really want (need) to hire you before they even know what it will cost them.

When the employer is invested in hiring you, the two of you share a common purpose: getting you hired. That means the two of you are now working together, *as partners,* to find a mutually satisfactory agreement. Focus your energy and the discussion on this, instead of playing "tug-of-war" over the issues.

FINDING A PERSONAL CONNECTION

Stop and ask yourself: Who do you trust? Who do you work well with? Who are you most comfortable with? The answer to all of these questions is probably the same: people similar to you, people who share your values and perspectives. This tells us that you can lower communication barriers—decrease defensiveness, anxiety, and fear (that awful "F" word again)—if you get the other side to see you as *someone more like them*.

Each of us has an identity—how we see ourselves, and how we want others to see us. We often surround ourselves with the symbols of that identity, such as pictures and books. A quick glance around your interviewer's office should reveal symbols of their identity.

We tend to trust and be comfortable with people who are like us. We want to work with people who are like us. **If you can find a personal connection to the other side, they will see you as someone like them, someone they can trust, and someone they would like to work with.**

Finding a personal connection can be as simple as, "I see you play golf—so do I." Do you have children? Do you have dogs? Do you like to sail or play tennis? Did we go to the same school? Have we lived in the same regions, states, or countries? Do we have any friends or hobbies in common?

SINCERITY AND CREDIBILITY

Enlisting the other side's help is the best way to start a negotiation because it makes an ally out of your only available adversary. However, enlisting the employer's help only works if your comments are credible, and your comments can only be credible if they are sincere. Don't acknowledge the employer's investment in you if you don't really appreciate it. Don't trumpet unique value you don't have to offer; and don't fake a personal connection if you can't find one. In other words, don't force it.

If you really mean it, enlisting the other side's help is the best way to get a negotiation exchange underway. However, if what you say isn't true, the other side probably will find you out, and you could lose more ground than you gain. In the end, your real goal is to lower barriers and reduce defensiveness. You want to get the other side working *with* you, and that won't happen if they think you aren't sincere and credible.

Managing the Flow of Information

Once you have enlisted the employer's help, the next step is to use that help to learn as much as you can about the employer's issues and interests so that you can add their side of the playing field to yours. At this point, your most important goals should be:

INFORMATION-GATHERING GOALS

- To determine what the *issues* are for the other side

- To identify the employer's *underlying interests*

- To understand the *weight and importance* that the employer attaches to the issues, as well as the employer's degree of flexibility

DETERMINE THEIR ISSUES

When the employer makes an offer, the contents of that offer tell you what the issues are in the eyes of the employer. **What the offer may not tell you is which issues the employer feels strongly about—which issues the employer values, and why.**

The offer also will not tell you which issues the employer sees as *negotiable*. This last point is particularly important. Whether an issue is important or not, it may be a policy of the company not to negotiate it. It is important to find out where movement in the offer is possible, where movement is not possible, and why.

At this point in the discussion, it is important to focus on clarifying what you are being offered and why. It is not yet time to counter the offer or to attempt to negotiate the terms. That's like shooting an arrow before you have a clear target. Once you shoot an arrow, you cannot take it back even if you shoot at the wrong target. There will be plenty of time to negotiate later. For now, focus on gathering information rather than on prematurely negotiating the deal.

IDENTIFY THEIR INTERESTS

Asking questions is often the best way to obtain the information you need to identify the employer's interests. If you have done a good job enlisting the employer's help, you will have melted some of his/her resistance to answering your questions. For issues that are important to you but have not been included in the offer, or are of lower value than you seek, two good questions to ask are "Why?" and "Why not?" If the salary seems too low, ask the employer to explain how it was arrived at—"Why this salary?" If a signing bonus is not included, you might ask, "Why was a signing bonus *not* included in the offer?" **Asking the "why" and "why not" questions helps you identify the real interests underlying the settlement options the employer has offered.** This would be a good time to use any outside information you gathered, such as what typical starting salaries are or what signing bonuses have historically been. You might raise the question, "What are others in the company with my background typically offered?"

Keep in mind, of course, that the other side may not have the issues or interests distinction in mind. Many employer's will not have consciously wrestled with what they are trying to accomplish beyond hiring you. In fact, your questions can help educate the employer about their own underlying interests. By refocusing attention on their underlying interests, you can make those interests the focus of the negotiation. The more you can focus the negotiation on what the employer is really after, the easier it is for you to identify issues and options that will satisfy *both* sides' underlying interests. Understanding the employer's underlying interests increases your flexibility for finding mutually satisfactory settlement options and, thereby, gives you a better chance to obtain the value you seek.

For example, what if the employer justifies your salary as "the same that all the new hires will receive this year"? That implies something important about the employer's interests. It implies that the employer may be interested in equity across all new hires. That doesn't mean that you can't get a better salary offer. It does mean that whatever salary offer you get may need to address this interest of the employer.

DETERMINE THEIR MOST/LEAST IMPORTANT ISSUES AND FLEXIBILITY

Understanding the employer's underlying interests is a good way to understand where movement isn't possible or likely. It is important to remember that negotiation is not about the issues. Negotiation is about the value we obtain from those issues. If an employer can't move on an issue, that is important to know. It means that you will have to find your value elsewhere.

Of course, understanding why the employer can't move on an issue may give you an insight into where movement is possible or even how you can make movement possible on that "non-negotiable" issue. It is important to understand the difference between won't and can't. "Won't" is usually a matter of choice. You should try to determine if there is something the employer values more that will induce him/her to change the "won't" to "will." "Can't" means that movement isn't possible. Sometimes, the "why" question reveals that the person you are talking to can't give you what you want, but someone else could! Maybe you can get that person involved in the negotiation.

Asking questions is also a good way to signal your interest in issues that are not yet on the table. Rather than saying, "I can't consider an offer that doesn't include moving expenses," try asking the question: "Is there some reason that moving expenses are not included in the offer?" Questions are easier to handle than demands and are less confrontational. Questions don't say "no" to the offer, even when they signal that other issues or options are of interest. They simply signal your interest in an undisclosed issue and test the employer's flexibility. The more issues you raise, the more opportunities you provide the employer to let you obtain value. In addition, the more issues you raise, the more opportunities you give yourself to find a mutually satisfactory agreement.

Taking Your Leave

Once you have enough information to understand the employer's issues and interests, you are ready to prepare your counteroffer. Begin by thanking the employer for the offer again. Then explain that you would like some time to consider the offer. Be sure to tell the employer when he/she can expect to receive your response.

Then go home, pat yourself on the back for a job well done, and get the celebrating out of your system. Find a comfortable place to work and start planning your strategy for countering the offer. Begin by comparing what you want (your side of the playing field) to what the employer has offered. You should complete your preference sheet by adding what you have learned about the employer's side of the playing field given the offer, your post-offer discussion, and your research.

The complete preference sheet will help you to determine *all* the issues in this negotiation, the likely settlement options for each issue, the value each side attaches to each issue and option, and the underlying interests that determine those values. This gives you a complete picture of the playing field for this negotiation. (It might even give you some hints about the playing field for your other negotiations!) Having done so, you can move on to applying the strategies available for expanding the pie and claiming more of its value for yourself.

- You don't obtain *anything* in a negotiation until the other side says, "Yes!"

- You can make the employer less defensive and less anxious by giving them something *right now* in return for their investment in you. You can give them your thanks for being considered.

- The first goal of any negotiation should be to enlist the assistance of the other side—to form a partnership to solve the problem, "How can we come to a mutually satisfying agreement?"

- The real exchange in this negotiation is between the value you bring to the job and the value the employer offers you. Focus on the *unique* value you bring to get them invested in hiring *you*.

- Asking questions is often the best way to get information about what is important to them, their flexibility and underlying interests, to signal your interest in issues that are not yet on the table.

- Take time to consider the offer and map out your negotiation strategy before you counter the offer.

4 SURVIVAL SKILL 1: EXPANDING THE PIE

The phone rang twice before it was picked up.

"Hi, Mom. It's Chris."

"Hi, Honey. What a treat to hear your voice in the middle of the day. Is something wrong?"

"No, no, no—nothing's wrong. It is just the opposite. I have a very interesting job offer. Well, sort of anyway. It is from Allied Products. But we're still working out the details, like salary. I called to tell you about it."

There was a pause. Chris could hear the concern in his mom's voice when she asked, "Has there been a problem at GCD Corporation, son? I thought you were really happy there."

"I was. I mean I am happy at GCD, Mom. It is just a good time for a new challenge," Chris said. "Sara and I agreed that I would go on the market when I finished up the evening M.B.A. program. She thought about doing the same before she got a promotion," he added.

"I guess that makes sense, dear. Have you let your boss know?" she asked.

"Yeah, in fact he made me a really good offer to stay. I'll make a decision after I negotiate the offer with Allied Products."

"That sounds good," she began slowly. "But do you really think it is wise to try to negotiate with Allied Products? You said it was a very interesting offer."

Chris pondered that for a moment. "I did say that, didn't I?" He chuckled. "But that doesn't mean that it couldn't be even better. There are still a lot of details we have not discussed yet. I would like to influence those details as much as possible, as constructively as possible."

"What details will you try to improve?" she asked with interest.

"Well, the amount of salary for one thing and a signing bonus for another. I talked to another graduate of my M.B.A. program who worked in their New York office. He was able to negotiate a $4,000 signing bonus. He said they don't negotiate vacation days though. The university placement director said the same thing."

"What does Sara think of all of this, Chris?"

"She thinks it's great. Because she's in consulting, her firm will let her live anywhere we decide, as long as we are near a major airport."

"That Sara is really something," his mom said with affection. "But what does she think about all of this negotiating?"

"Mom, remember who we are talking about here. Compared to Sara, I will take it easy on them. In fact, she has suggested that I ask them to pay our moving expenses if they send me to another city."

Mom was silent again. "Gee, dear, I assumed they would decide all that."

Chris smiled. "Yes, Mom—they will if I let them."

When it comes to making offers and counteroffers in a negotiation, both employer and applicant are trying to do as well as possible. Each wants to leave the negotiation with as much as possible. There's nothing wrong with that. In fact, that's the point of negotiation. **Whether you are an applicant or an employer, the goal of negotiation is to claim as much value as possible for yourself.**

The problem in negotiation is that in most cases both sides cannot get everything they want. Employers would like to hire new applicants for nothing, but applicants (most anyway) are not willing to work for nothing. Applicants, on the other hand, would like an unlimited salary—but no employer is going to write a "blank check" to hire someone. Since neither side can get exactly what it wants, the goal of negotiation is for employer and applicant to find an "acceptable middle ground"—a point where both sides are willing to say yes, or even better, a point where both sides are *happy* to say yes. **Most negotiators make a costly mistake in negotiation when they assume that finding an acceptable middle ground means meeting in the middle—an equal split, or a compromise.**

We will tell you why this is such a costly assumption, how to avoid it, and what to do instead. To start, we will explain how this assumption is based on a myth: the myth of the fixed pie.

The Myth of the "Fixed Pie"

WHAT WOULD YOU DO?

Imagine that an employer has $80,000 left in the budget for next year and needs to hire an additional manager. He would like to hire a new manager for nothing and keep that $80,000 in reserve for next year to spend on other things. At the very least, he wants $20,000 in reserve for next year. An applicant would like to be paid as much as possible—certainly, all $80,000 if possible, but he/she would accept as little as $55,000.

Neither side is likely to get exactly what they want: The applicant is not going to take nothing, and the employer is not willing to spend all $80,000 on the applicant. Each will need to give something to find that middle ground where both are happy to say yes. The question is, what is that something?

Both seem willing to give a little. However, given $5,000 for benefits, $5,000 for reimbursed moving expenses, and $20,000 in reserve, the most the employer could offer is $50,000 in salary. The applicant wants $55,000—the employer only has $50,000 to offer.

It appears that there is no "middle ground" here—no salary figure that would make both employer and applicant happy. If the employer moves the applicant's salary offer up to $55,000, that will leave the employer less than $20,000 in reserve for next year. If the applicant accepts the $50,000 offer, the applicant will not make the minimum amount he/she requires. Now what?

If no acceptable middle ground is evident to you in the case above, it's probably due to your assumption that this negotiation is about a "fixed pie." **A fixed pie is a fixed amount of resources that the employer and applicant divide up.** If the amount of resources is fixed, the only way for the applicant to do better is for the employer to do worse, and vice versa. Both seem unable to get what they want because the employer can only *win* if the applicant accepts less than $55,000; the applicant can only *win* if the employer is willing to have less than $20,000 in reserve. Without negotiation training, this scenario would probably end with the applicant turning down the employer's job offer.

Expand the Pie to Create Value

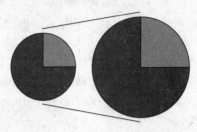

Fortunately for negotiators, appearances can be deceiving. Imagine that the employer and applicant could discover another $5,000—just through negotiating with each other. If they could find another $5,000, the applicant could make $55,000 next year, and the employer would have $20,000 in reserve. If they could do this, they would have *created* as well as claimed value through effective negotiation. Having done so, they could both get what they want and happily say yes.

WHY COMPROMISE IS A BAD IDEA

Expanding the pie is about finding ways to increase the value that can be divided between the two sides. If there is more value to go around—more for the employer and applicant to divide—then there is an opportunity for one or even *both* sides to do better. Most negotiators treat negotiation like a tug-of-war over a fixed pie. As a result, they miss important opportunities to expand the pie. When negotiators think they are arguing over a fixed pie, they may try to meet the other side halfway—to *compromise*. Many people think they are good negotiators because they know how to meet the other side halfway. **Compromise is not always a good strategy** because a compromise strategy may keep you from expanding the pie.

How can negotiators expand the pie? How can negotiators find more to go around, just through the process of negotiating? There are three basic principles to remember:

Principles to Help You Expand the Pie

- Be *firm* regarding the value you want but *flexible* in terms of how you get it.

- Distinguish the issues of greatest importance to you from those that are less important.

- Determine which of your important issues are less important to the employer and vise versa.

Be Firm on Value and Flexible on Form of the Agreement

The form of a job offer matters less than the value it represents. **Would you accept a job offer with no salary?** Your answer should be, "It depends." It depends on what else the offer includes. It depends on whether you are offered something else that provides you the same, or more, value. It is not the salary that is important. The best offer, whether it includes salary or not, is the one that provides the most overall value. It is up to you to negotiate what resources or issues that value comes from.

57

To do this, be flexible about the form of the agreement but firm about the amount of value you receive.

DISTINGUISH IMPORTANT FROM UNIMPORTANT ISSUES

In chapter 2, you created a "preference sheet" in which you weighted each issue and each option according to how important each was to you. In real life, value is not always easy to measure or even understand. Value may just be the "gut feeling" that one issue option is preferred to another option, even if you don't know why. The key here is that most applicants do not value all issues equally. The fact that you place different value on objectively equivalent issues (like that $5,000 in moving expenses) gives you a way to "expand the pie." **If you don't place much value on an issue, you can give ground on that issue in exchange for receiving concessions on an issue that you value more.** Objectively, the offer will be the same to the employer, but its *value* to you will have increased.

A review of table 4.1 will help us illustrate this way to "expand the pie."

This applicant includes two issues on her preference sheet: **Tuition Reimbursement** and **Moving-Expense Coverage.** However, she has assigned tuition-reimbursement dollars more value because she has few possessions and a large student loan to repay. For her, each $1,000 of tuition reimbursement is worth 1,000 points of value, while each $1,000 of moving expense money is worth only 100 points. This means the applicant will receive 1,000 more points of value for every $1,000 in tuition reimbursement she can get and only 100 points of value for every $1,000 in moving expenses. As a consequence, she

Table 4.1
Applicant Preference Sheet on Two Issues

Issue	Settlement Options	Value to Applicant
Moving-Expense Coverage	$1,000	100
	$2,000	200
	$3,000	300
	$4,000	400
	$5,000	500
Tuition Reimbursement	$1,000	1,000
	$2,000	2,000
	$3,000	3,000
	$4,000	4,000
	$5,000	5,000

would be better off if she trades her moving-expense dollars for additional tuition reimbursement.

Distinguish Your Issues from the Employer's Issues

Just as you value some issues more than others, some issues will be more valuable to the employer than others. Sometimes this is because it is easier for the employer to get money for some things than for others. For example, it may be easier for the employer to give you moving-expense money than signing-bonus money (or to give you signing-bonus money if he/she calls it moving-expense money!). That means that there are trade-offs that will increase the employer's value, just as there are trade-offs that will increase your value.

If both the employer and the applicant value tuition reimbursement dollars more than moving expense dollars, there are no trade-offs that will expand the pie. As you will see when you review the preference sheet in table 4.2, in that case a trade that is good (increases value) for the applicant will hurt the employer and vice versa.

When both sides prefer the same issues, there are no trades that increase the value for both sides or expand the pie. Notice that in this example the amount of value shared by the applicant and employer is the same regardless of the agreement reached. **However two sides in a negotiation rarely prefer the same issues.** As a consequence, they can almost always do bet-

TABLE 4.2 APPLICANT AND EMPLOYER PREFERENCES ON TWO ISSUES
A "FIXED PIE": NO TRADE-OFFS ARE POSSIBLE

Issue	Settlement Options	Value to Applicant	Value to Employer
Moving-Expense Coverage	$1,000	100	500
	$2,000	200	400
	$3,000	300	300
	$4,000	400	200
	$5,000	500	100
Tuition Reimbursement	$1,000	1,000	5,000
	$2,000	2,000	4,000
	$3,000	3,000	3,000
	$4,000	4,000	2,000
	$5,000	5,000	1,000

ter than compromising and meeting halfway. A good example is provided in table 4.3.

TABLE 4.3 APPLICANT AND EMPLOYER PREFERENCES ON TWO ISSUES MAKING TRADE-OFFS THAT EXPAND THE PIE

Issue	Settlement Options	Value to Applicant	Value to Employer
Moving-Expense Coverage	$1,000	100	5,000
	$2,000	200	4,000
	$3,000	300	3,000
	$4,000	400	2,000
	$5,000	500	1,000
Tuition Reimbursement	$1,000	1,000	500
	$2,000	2,000	400
	$3,000	3,000	300
	$4,000	4,000	200
	$5,000	5,000	100

Here, the applicant cares more about getting tuition reimbursement and the employer cares more about restricting moving expenses.

The maximum either party could receive is 5,500 points of value (5,000 points on the more important issue, and 500 points on the less important issue). If they compromise (meet halfway on both issues), they will split 6,600 points of value, 3,300 points each. However, if they each trade their least important issue for their most important issue, they can expand the pie and split 10,000 points—fully 5,000 points apiece. That means that you can often get more value out of what is objectively the same offer (in dollars), by making trades that help both sides. **When we expand the pie, we do not change the resources that the two sides bring to the table. What we change is the form of that value and as a consequence the amount of *value* that the two sides divide. Expanding the pie means dividing the same resources in ways that create larger amounts of value for the negotiators to divide.** A compromise is often a missed opportunity to make a trade that helps both sides.

The best negotiators understand that giving up value does not have to imply compromise. It can mean trading off issues so that when you give up value, you get back more in return. **The best negotiations occur when both sides get back more than they give.** That's what *expanding the pie* is all about.

Let's apply these concepts to the example we described at the beginning of the chapter. You'll recall that the applicant has been offered $50,000, but wants $55,000. If the applicant anticipates few moving expenses (a low-value issue), the applicant could offer to trade the $5,000 moving expenses reimbursement in exchange for a $5,000 pay increase. This would still leave the employer $20,000 in reserve for next year, while providing the applicant the desired $55,000 salary. Both sides get more of what they want by recognizing that $1,000 on some issues is more valuable than $1,000 on other issues. They expand the pie by finding more value to go around.

The more questions you ask, the more opportunities you have for helping the employer identify issues and trades that meet his/her underlying interests and provide you more value. Also, the better you will be able to understand and define the employer's side of the playing field and how it relates to your own.

HOW TO TRADE ISSUES TO EXPAND THE PIE

- Identify trades that enhance your value, at no cost to the employer.

- Identify trades that enhance the employer's value, at no cost to you.

- Identify trades that enhance value for both sides.

The best trades are those that allow both sides to claim more.

More Strategies for Expanding the Pie

In addition to making strategic trade-offs, there are three other strategies for expanding the pie:

MORE STRATEGIES FOR EXPANDING THE PIE

- Fractioning issues
- Compatible issues
- Adding issues

FRACTIONING ISSUES

Sometimes applicants miss opportunities to expand the pie because they see issues as wholes, rather than as parts that create a whole. *Fractioning the issue*—splitting it into subissues—can provide opportunities to identify issues that the two sides value differently.

The classic example of fractioning issues comes from the story of the two sisters and an orange. It seems that there were two sisters. One wanted to bake a cake and the other wanted to make some marmalade. Both needed an orange—but there was only one orange in the house, and they couldn't both have it. They were arguing about who deserved to get it when one sister mentioned that she had her heart set on using the *fruit* of the orange to make her marmalade. All argument stopped at that point because the sister baking the cake realized that she needed only the peel of the orange to bake the cake. This meant that while there might be only one orange, neither sister needed all of it. One sister valued the peel and not the fruit; one sister valued the fruit and not the peel. By fractioning the issue—in this case, fractioning the orange into peel and fruit—they found a way for both of them to get everything that they wanted. They turned a tug-of-war over what they thought was a fixed pie into a winning agreement for both sides.

Fractioning can be a useful approach to dealing with many issues that appear to present a tug-of-war. A marketing job in Boston, for example, consists of two subissues: a job in Boston, and a job in marketing. Just because the employer offers you a marketing job in Boston doesn't mean that the employer is equally committed to your being assigned to marketing and to your going to Boston. If you can learn which aspect of the job—that the job is in Boston, or that the job is in marketing—is more important to the employer, you may be able to negotiate each one separately. If the real issue for the employer is location (there are only openings in Boston) but the real issue for the applicant is the function (a job in finance), a bridging solution would be a finance job in Boston. Bridging the two parts of a fractioned issue is a way to create a compatible issue—a single issue that contains a trade that helps both sides.

Compatible Issues

Another way to enhance value in a negotiation is to recognize *compatible issues.* An issue is compatible when both sides prefer the same option. An example of a compatible issue—*Starting Date*—is shown in table 4.4. The applicant prefers the earliest starting date (she wants to start making money) and

Table 4.4
A Compatible issue: *Starting Date*

Settlement Options	Value to Applicant	Value to Employer
June 1	1,500	1,500
July 1	1,000	1,000
August 1	500	500
September 1	0	0

June 1st is the mutually satisfactory resolution.

surprise . . . the employer also prefers the earliest starting date (the employer needs the applicant to start work as soon as possible).

Compatible issues should be easy to manage because both sides want the same thing. Of course, before they can agree to what they both want, they have to realize it's what they both want. **The "fixed-pie bias" often prevents negotiators from realizing that their preferences on a particular issue really are compatible.** When this happens they sometimes get what they both don't want. How does this happen? The fixed-pie bias leads negotiators to use two strategies that prevent them from identifying compatible issues.

First, the fixed-pie bias leads negotiators to misrepresent what they want. (We will talk more about misrepresentation in chapter 6). When negotiators misrepresent their interests, they may never discover that they want the same thing. Second, when negotiators really want a deal, their first bid will often be a compromise offer. For example, an employer who wants a June 1 start date may offer June 15 instead, as a sign of commitment and good will. Since this is so close to what the applicant wants, the applicant may simply agree—without ever realizing that there is a starting date that is better for *both* sides. Thus, neither party gets what they want because they miss the compatible issue.

It is important to note that when negotiator preferences are compatible, they are not distributing a fixed pie. In this example, if the applicant and the employer agree to a July 1 start date (which neither prefers), each will realize 1,000 points of value, and together they will be distributing a pie of 2,000 points. In contrast, if the applicant and the employer agree to a June 1 start date (which both prefer), each will realize 1,500 units of value, and together they will be distributing a pie of 3,000 units of value. This is no tug-of-war over a fixed pie. Instead, they enlarge the pie by settling on an option that allows both of them to do their best.

ADDING ISSUES:
DON'T NEGOTIATE ONE ISSUE AT A TIME

Negotiators cannot make trades that help both sides when they are discussing only one issue. To make trades that expand the pie, negotiators have to discuss two or more issues—an important one to receive and a less important one to give away. The more issues discussed simultaneously—the more issues "on the table" at the same time—the more likely you are to find issues to trade.

An employer may try to negotiate one issue at a time. Some will even push you to agree to an offer on one issue before he/she will discuss another. Remember that the goal is not the value you obtain from a particular issue but the *overall* value you obtain from the package. Unless the employer offers so much on one issue that the rest are moot, you cannot determine the value of the offer from one issue. Moreover, you cannot know whether an offer on one issue is a good offer until you know how much value it is going to cost you on other issues. If an employer wants to negotiate with you one issue at a time, we advise that you:

IF THE EMPLOYER NEGOTIATES ONE ISSUE AT A TIME

- Explain that what you get on one issue is less important than what you get on the overall package.

- Point out that there may be many combinations of the issues that would make a good package for you.

- Suggest a couple of trades that might be good for both of you.

- Consider agreeing "tentatively" on an issue if it looks good relative to your target for that issue. Do so with the understanding that you may revisit the issue later, in light of new information about the rest of the package.

Negotiating one issue at a time closes off opportunities to expand the pie and obtain more value. Only by getting multiple issues on the table can you make trades that help both sides get closer to agreement.

It is particularly important to avoid negotiating one issue at a time at the beginning of a negotiation. One-issue discussions always turn into a tug-of-war—unless that one issue happens to be a compatible one! At the beginning of a negotiation, negotiating one issue at a time can set a negative tone for things that follow. This makes it much harder to use the strategies you are learning in this book!

Help the Employer Help You

You don't have to like the other side in a negotiation for expanding the pie to make sense. Expanding the pie is a good tactic even if you are unconcerned about making friends or whether the other side does well. **Expanding the pie makes sense because helping the other side do well is often the best way to do well yourself.**

If the employer does well, they are more likely to agree to what you want. Expanding the pie often does mean giving something up. But if done correctly, it also means getting more in return and helping the employer agree to what you want. Therefore, the best reason to expand the pie is to do well yourself. Three good things happen when you help the employer do well:

REASONS TO EXPAND THE PIE

- You do better because the employer can afford to give you more value when they get more value.

- You are more likely to get an agreement because they are more likely to say yes to your offer.

- The next negotiation may be easier because you have shown the other side it is possible for *both* of you to do well.

Expanding the pie and creating value does not make much sense unless you claim as much as possible of the value you have identified. Expanding the pie doesn't make the task of claiming value go away—it just makes it easier.

- "Expanding the pie" means finding more value to go around in a negotiation.

- The best offer is the one that offers you the most total value.

- The fact that you value objectively equivalent issues differently gives you a way to expand the pie. You expand the pie when you make trades that help both sides.

- A compromise is often a missed opportunity to make a trade that helps both sides. Only use compromise when there does not appear to be a trade-off.

- You also expand the pie whenever you identify and agree on options that are compatible.

- Expanding the pie makes sense in negotiations because helping the other side is often the best way to help yourself.

- The final goal of any negotiation should always be to claim as much value as you can for yourself.

- Sometimes negotiators miss opportunities to expand the pie when they don't fraction issues into subissues that the two sides value differently.

5 SURVIVAL SKILL 2: CLAIMING VALUE

Chris took a deep breath and began. "I hope you know that I am as anxious to work toward an agreement as you are. I am hopeful that we can create a contract that will work for both of us. After all, we are on the same page. We would both like me to be able to accept this exceptional opportunity."

"That's terrific, Chris. I am glad to hear it." Mr. Burton leaned forward and smiled. "Does that mean you are ready to accept our offer?"

"I can promise to give you a definitive answer the next time we speak, but I have a couple of questions I would like to ask first, if I may," Chris added.

"Sure, Chris, what would you like to know?"

"After I received your offer, I felt obligated to inform my current employer that I was considering a move. The truth is that I was surprised and gratified when my boss came back to me with a counteroffer. I remain, however, very serious about the prospect of coming to work for you."

"I am relieved to hear it," Mr. Burton said.

Chris smiled and then continued. "I do want to make a careful, well-informed decision, so I want to be completely clear about the specifics of your offer. I have some questions about the contract I received in writing this week from your Human Resources people. While the salary is good, it falls at about the midpoint of the market for similar positions in this industry. I think you would agree that my skill set, experience, education, and past performance all put me in the top 10 percent or so of the market. I was hoping for a salary commensurate with that assessment. I was hoping for a salary of $60,000." Chris stopped and summoned his courage before adding with more confidence than he felt, "Is that possible?"

**AFTER YOU READ THIS CHAPTER,
YOU'LL KNOW:**

- How to claim more for yourself without jeopardizing the relationship

- How to make the other side want what you give them when you can't give them what they want

- Why making the first move can get you more of what you want

- How to make the *right* first move

Claiming More for Ourselves

Successful negotiating is about claiming value for yourself. We expand the pie because it makes it easier to claim value for ourselves, by making it easier to give the other side what they need to reach an agreement. **When we can't expand the pie and we can't give the other side what they want, we can still negotiate successfully by helping the other side want what we give them.**

People would like to get it all—to get their preferred option on all issues. The next best thing to getting it all is to give less ground. When the issues seem to present a "fixed pie," the right strategy is to make the other side think they didn't lose (or even won) the negotiation. Making the other side think they won a negotiation has two aspects: altering the other side's perception of what *they* got and altering the other side's perception of what

75

you got. Both of these can be accomplished through *justified anchoring.*

Help Them Want What You Give Them

ANCHORING

Anchoring occurs when a reference point alters a negotiator's belief about how much he/she can successfully claim in a negotiation.

Take the example of the $5,000 available as a signing bonus. The applicant will want as much as possible of the money available for signing bonuses. When the applicant does not know how much is available (which is typical) the applicant will try to *estimate* how much is available. The applicant's estimate will be quite different if the employer's initial offer is a $1,000 signing bonus than if the employer's initial offer is $4,000. **The initial offer will anchor the applicant's beliefs about what is possible and therefore about what is a fair outcome, a good outcome, or even a winning outcome for the applicant.**

If the applicant is initially offered a $1,000 signing bonus, an offer of $2,000 may look fabulous—a 100 percent increase over the initial offer! On the other hand, if the applicant is initially offered a $4,000 signing bonus, an offer of $5,000 may seem like only a modest (20 percent) improvement. In the end, the applicant getting the $2,000 signing bonus may feel better about "winning" the negotiation than the applicant getting the $5,000 signing bonus—even though $5,000 is much more money.

JUSTIFICATION

Anchoring works best when a justification is given for the anchor. **Providing justification legitimates an anchor.** Imagine that the employer offers the applicant a $1,000 signing bonus, accompanied by the comment that "$1,000 is what this firm has always given new hires as a signing bonus." **Justified anchoring makes the negotiation not just about the amount but also about why the amount is fair and correct.** Justification can make negotiators feel that they claimed as much as they could and therefore got a good outcome—even if they did not.

Making the First Move

It is not uncommon for an employer to ask you for a "recommendation" before putting pen to paper. The employer might ask you, "So what do you think would be an appropriate offer?" The employer might ask you to make the first move. How should you respond to this opportunity?

You should avoid this discussion until you have sold the employer on you—on the value you can bring to the company. You would like the employer to be committed to hiring you *before* the two of you discuss how much it will cost. The more value the employer believes you offer, the more value you should be able to ask for—and get!

But once you know you have sold the employer on yourself, should you be willing to make a recommendation? Should you be willing to make the first bid? Many job applicants are reluctant to make the first move. They are afraid that if they make the first bid, one of two things will happen:

> ## APPLICANTS DON'T MAKE THE
> ## FIRST MOVE BECAUSE:
>
> ■ They will ask for *too little*—less than the employer would have offered—and they will get the job for less value than they could have.
>
> ■ They will ask for *too much*—more than the employer is willing to pay—and the employer will lose interest in hiring them.

Both of these seem to be reasonable concerns—but they are also avoidable if you make the first move *after* you are offered the job! When you don't make the first move, you lose an important strategic opportunity.

Making the first move gives you an important opportunity to play the game on your playing field. When you make the first move, you *anchor* the negotiation to your advantage in two important ways: First, you anchor the other side's thinking about the *numbers* when you put the first number on the table. Second, the justification you make anchors the discussion about what the "right" number should be *and why*.

Let's say you make the following suggestion:

"I think a reasonable salary offer would be about $60,000—because that's what similarly qualified graduates of my M.B.A. program were offered by other companies this year."

You have focused the discussion around the number $60,000—*your* number—and whether $60,000 is the right number or not. And you have (implicitly) asked the employer to *disprove* your justification if the employer wants you to accept something lower. Your $60,000 "suggestion" and the justification you offered for it are the starting point—the anchors—for the discussion that follows. That means you are playing the game on your playing field, and that means you will do better.

But how do you avoid the two problems—the two fears—about suggesting too little and suggesting too much? These fears are unfounded if you following three simple rules:

RULES FOR MAKING THE FIRST MOVE

- If asked to make the first bid, do so only after you have been offered the job.

- Always suggest an amount that will make you happy if they say yes.

- Only suggest what you can justify. You never want to have the employer ask you "Where did you come up with that number?" and not have a strong justification for it.

You should be aggressive and provide a justification that offers you more value. If you have done your homework, an aggressive suggestion—that can be justified—should keep you "in the ballpark" *and* prevent you from asking for too little. Even if you aggressively suggest more than the employer was considering, a reasonable justification will keep you from sounding greedy and should keep the discussion open. This opens the discussion at *your* starting point.

When you make the first move, don't forget that you are after value, and the value you obtain comes from the *entire* package, not just one or two issues. When you make the first move, the suggestion you make should be a suggested *package*—including aggressive settlement options for your most important issues—not just a suggested settlement option for a single issue.

- If you can't give the other side what they want, you can use *anchoring* and *justification* to make the other side want what you give them.

- Making the first offer gets the game started on your playing field, where you are more likely to win.

- Make the first bid only after you are offered the job.

- When you make the first bid, ask for enough to be happy if they say yes. Only ask for what you can justify.

6 RESPONDING TO OFFERS

"Wow, Chris, $60,000 would be quite an increase over your current salary, now wouldn't it? I will have to look into this and get back to you." Mr. Burton drummed his fingers on the desk and looked directly into Chris's eyes.

Chris returned the direct look and said, "I would very much appreciate your doing that, Mr. Burton. Thanks. Thanks also for arranging for me to receive the marketing position in Chicago. As you know, that was my first choice."

"I am glad that we were able to make that work. Are there any other issues?"

"Just a few. Perhaps we could talk about moving-expense coverage. Given the bids I have received, I think your offer on moving expenses will cover only 50 percent of our costs. We are cash poor so this could be a real hardship." Chris stopped and waited for Mr. Burton's response. After ninety seconds Chris almost gave up and withdrew the request, but stopped himself just in time.

Finally Mr. Burton said, "I am sorry, Chris, but I have little flexibility on this issue. We give a standard package to all our employees to handle their moves. Even I was unable to get more when I joined the company."

"I see," said Chris. "Perhaps we could find an alternative way to cover some of these expenses. What about increasing the signing bonus?"

"We could definitely do that, but not enough to cover the remaining 50 percent in moving expenses," Mr. Burton added with a shrug.

"I am disappointed but I understand. I am just not sure that I will be able to swing it. This move will also mean a change in position for my spouse, and I have a large student loan to repay."

"Would it help for us to pay off your student loan?" inquired Mr. Burton.

"That would be great," Chris answered.

Once you have learned as much as you can about what the employer values and what is possible, it is time to put it all together in order to expand the pie and claim value for yourself. It is time to respond to the employer's offer by **making a counteroffer.** First, we consider how to respond to **"exploding offers"** or how to stop the employer from forcing you to decide before you know everything you want to know. Then we discuss three important tactics to use in making effective counteroffers:

> ## Tactics for Effective Counteroffers
>
> - Lead with your target.
>
> - Package to expand the pie.
>
> - Justify your requests.

Exploding Offers: How to Avoid a Job Mine

A short fuse or "exploding offer" on a deadline sometimes accompanies an offer. This deadline can be inconvenient when you are in the midst of the interview process and waiting on other offers.

Organizations use exploding offers and other pressure tactics for two reasons: First, exploding offers increase the probability that you will accept their offer since exploding offers limit your opportunity to obtain competing offers. Second, exploding offers reduce the likelihood that the employer will lose their second-choice applicant because you waited a long time before rejecting their offer.

Applicants face a dilemma when they receive an exploding offer while waiting for a (potentially more attractive) offer from a different employer. They can accept the offer in hand, and thus forego any further search for a better alternative. Or they can pass up the offer in hand, risking the possibility that this will be their only offer. Either decision spells lost opportunity and must be avoided.

We suggest you use the following four-step process to deal with exploding offers.

> ## HOW TO DIFFUSE AN EXPLODING OFFER
>
> ■ Ask the recruiter to explain the deadline.
>
> ■ Ask the recruiter to postpone the deadline.
>
> ■ Inform alternative organizations about your short fuse.
>
> ■ Use the Farpoint Gambit.

First, ask the employer to explain the reason for the short time period and specific deadline. You may be able to identify an alternative that alleviates the employer's concerns and extends the time period. Strive to make a trade that will help both sides avoid the deadline.

Second, try to get the employer to postpone the deadline. Tell the employer that you would like to postpone the decision until you have had the opportunity to explore all of your options. Explain that this does not imply a lack of interest in their offer, only that you wish to make a careful decision that will hopefully allow you to accept their offer with certainty. Then propose a specific alternative decision date.

Third, inform your potential alternatives about your short fuse. Ask about the status of your application and determine the possibility of getting a decision from them before your impending deadline. If possible, pursue your alternatives before the deadline.

If all else fails, take the final step and use the *Farpoint Gambit*. The Farpoint Gambit was derived from an episode of *Star Trek: The Next Generation* in which Captain Picard and his crew were put on trial by a powerful alien civilization. At one point during the trial, the alien judge said, "Bailiff, if the next word out of the defendant's mouth is anything but guilty, kill him." Picard thought for a moment and then replied, "Guilty . . . provisionally." He then went on to explain the provision, having constructively turned the table on the judge. You should do the same.

To use the Farpoint Gambit, carefully consider the offer and what it would take (if anything) to make it acceptable. If nothing would make the offer acceptable, turn it down. If you know what it would take for you to say yes right now, use the Farpoint Gambit as follows:

"I would prefer to have more time. By taking away that time, you have reduced my options. While I understand your need for doing so, it creates a real dilemma for me. I have decided to accept your offer if you can compensate me by improving the offer in the following manner. Providing you can deal with these remaining issues, I accept your offer . . . provisionally."

LEAD WITH YOUR TARGETS

Once you have forestalled any exploding offers, it is time to make a counteroffer. In many negotiations, your counteroffer represents your first opportunity to suggest settlement options.

Remember that the employer's first offer provided a chance to anchor you. Now your counteroffer provides a chance for you to anchor the employer. **It makes sense to lead with your targets, the settlement option you prefer on each issue, even if you don't think you'll get them.**

YOU SHOULD LEAD WITH YOUR TARGET BECAUSE:

- It lets them know what you really want.

- It allows them to see where you are making concessions.

In the give-and-take of a negotiation, the employer can't give you what you really want if he/she doesn't know what it is. Don't begin your counteroffer with a compromise. Don't begin with a settlement option below your target because it seems too far above the initial offer made by the employer. If you do this, you will have made a unilateral concession and received nothing in return. In addition, you will have guaranteed that you will not make your target.

Targets should always be high but defensible. High targets will anchor the negotiation in a favorable way to you, but only if you present a figure that you can justify. Unrealistic targets make a very poor impression on the employer and can derail the negotiation altogether.

Targets should never be made in the form of a range. A range provides both a top end and bottom figure. Ranges that truthfully represent both your target and bottom line provide the other side a dangerously low anchor (your bottom line). You are likely to elicit an offer that just exceeds your bottom line. Ranges that are strategically high but inaccurate or indefensible are likely to be rejected.

When an employer rejects an unrealistically high range, you have less than ideal reaction choices. You can walk away since the offer is lower than your purported (but false) bottom line and give up value. Or you can accept an offer below your purported bottom line, while acknowledging that it did not reflect your true requirements. In this second case, it is unrealistic to expect the employer to trust you further. Avoid both problems by presenting only your target and not your bottom line. **You cannot get what you do not ask for. It is fine to make a strong counteroffer as long as you can justify it and present it professionally as a request or question and not a demand.** Leading with your target also allows the employer to see where you are making concessions and frame the offer.

HOW TO FRAME THE OFFER

Helping the employer see where you make concessions is a way to **frame** the employer. **Framing is the process of getting the other side to see your offer as a gain to them rather than a loss.** Research has shown that negotiators avoid the risk of impasse by making more concessions when they think they have **gains** to protect. However, they are willing to risk impasse by making fewer concessions to avoid **losses.** You can influence whether they see your counteroffer as a gain or as a loss.

Imagine you told an employer that you were looking for a $70,000 salary, but that you would be willing to "settle for" $65,000. You are offering the employer a $5,000 concession on salary—a gain for the employer over what you were looking for. In negotiation, it's always a risk to say no to an offer and keep negotiating. But the employer can protect the $5,000 concession he/she's "won"—ground already gained—just by saying, "OK, I agree." There's no risk for the employer in saying yes.

If you "frame" your concessions with gain language ("I would be willing to accept $65,000, which is $5,000 less than the $70,000 I am after") as opposed to loss language ("I would be willing to accept $65,000, which is $5,000 more than you are offering") the employer will be more likely to accept the concessions you have made and say yes to your requests.

PACKAGE ISSUES

It should be clear by now that we collect information in order to identify opportunities to expand the pie. As we saw in chapter 4, expanding the pie makes it easier to give the other side what they want and enhance the value you can claim for yourself.

As we also noted in chapter 4, you cannot expand the pie if you are only discussing one issue. You need to be discussing two (or more!) issues—or two or more parts of an issue—to be able to make a trade that helps both sides. This leads to a simple but critical rule in making counteroffers: **Never make unilateral concessions. If you are going to make a concession (for example, lower your salary target from $70,000 to $65,000), always ask for something in exchange.** For example, in exchange for accepting that $5,000 decrease in salary, ask for more moving expenses.

If you have done a good job collecting information about

what the other side values, you can package your concessions with requests on issues that you value more than the employer. If you place more value on moving expenses than the employer does, an equivalent trade between moving expenses and salary will be a trade that claims more value for you.

Of course, even your best efforts to collect information may not tell you exactly which package would be the most attractive to the employer. **Be prepared to propose several possible packages.** Offer to accept a lower salary in exchange for more moving expenses. If the recruiter declines, remember to respond with a question such as "Why?" or "Why not?" Then you can follow up with another package that allows you to address the concern—such as an earlier-than-normal performance review, a salary adjustment, or perhaps a company car.

By proposing several different packages, you let the employer find the package that offers the company the most value. As long as all the packages are good for you—as long as they all increase the value you claim—it shouldn't matter to you which package they prefer. If the employer does like one of the packages you have proposed, that means the package claims more value for them. In addition, that means you have expanded the pie and moved one step closer to agreement.

Use Accounts to Justify Your Requests

An important element of the counteroffer process is justifying your requests or targets—explaining *why* you want what you want. Justifications like these are known as **accounts.** Providing accounts that justify or explain your requests can help you in three important ways:

THE BENEFITS OF USING ACCOUNTS

- Accounts that refer to *your own interests* offer the employer an opportunity to expand the pie.

- Accounts that refer to *the employer's* underlying interests help him/her realize that your request increases the value the company claims.

- Accounts that refer to an external justification for your request provide you an opportunity to claim value.

When the account that you give refers to *your own interests,* your account offers the employer an opportunity to expand the pie.

Imagine, for example, that you offer the following account:

"According to my calculations, I need at least $3,000 in moving expenses in order to be able to move here."

What you have explained with this account is your underlying interest—I need money up-front in order to be able to move to this job. That underlying interest is what is driving your request for $3,000 in moving expenses.

When you identify your underlying interests, you make it possible for the other side to find ways other than your request to satisfy those underlying interests. In this case, if the company is unable to provide moving expenses, they could address your underlying interest with a salary advance, or a short-term, low-interest loan.

Your underlying interests represent the real value for you in the negotiation. If your accounts help the other side understand your underlying interests, those accounts can also help the other side satisfy your underlying interests.

An account that refers to the *employer's underlying interests* may help the employer realize that your request actually increases the value the company claims.

The other side's underlying interests represent the real value for them in the negotiation, so an account can show them how what you want is in their best interests. Imagine, for example, that you offer the following account:

"I would be willing to accept a lower salary in exchange for more moving expenses because it sounds like you have more flexibility on moving expenses than on salary."

By referring to the underlying interests driving their offer (i.e., salary is a more important issue for the employer than moving expenses), you encourage the employer to see that the package you are offering increases the value they are claiming. In addition, this account offers a trade that helps you, but sounds like you are making a concession.

When the account you give provides an external justification for your request, your account provides you an opportunity to claim value.

Remember that we negotiate because we are not sure what the right answer is. An external justification offers objective evidence of what the right answer is and, therefore, may convince the employer that you deserve what you want. Imagine, for example, that you offer the following account:

> *"I would like $3,000 in moving expenses because that's what other companies are offering to applicants with my experience and performance record."*

This account places the burden on the employer to explain why you should not get $3,000 in moving expenses. External accounts anchor the other side and frame anything less than what you want as a concession you have made.

In formulating an external account, realize that there may be multiple ways to arrive at the "right answer"—many ways to put together evidence at hand to create an objective standard. Don't be afraid to use the most favorable standard available for your account. However, make sure the standard you use is defensible, because you may have to defend it. If the best applicants are getting salaries in the $70,000 range, keep that as your justification for getting a salary that is similar. However, if those offers are in a different field, or are for jobs that you wouldn't take, they won't provide a very convincing standard and may not help your case.

Another reasonable and advantageous standard is **your best alternative offer:**

> *"I want to be as straightforward with you as possible. While I am delighted with your offer and the prospect of working with you, I think you should know that another company has made me an offer that includes significantly more salary. Is there room for flexibility in your offer?"*

Your current position can also provide a standard. Let's say you are looking for a salary increase of 10–15 percent over your current salary. You might provide the following account:

"I think this could be a terrific opportunity for me and hope that we can make it work, but given all of the transitions we are talking about for my family, I think a salary increase of 15 percent is warranted. Is this possible?"

Accounts should not be about conning the other side. Accounts should be about using objective evidence to convince them that you deserve what you are requesting. Before you select the appropriate standard to use in this negotiation, consider carefully which ones could be advantageous, while also convincing and objectively defensible.

In the final analysis, you don't have to justify what you want and you don't have to say yes if they don't give it to you. However, you are much more likely to get what you want if you can offer an account that makes sense. Offering an account creates a dialogue about what is the right offer and why, without merely accepting or declining the offer as is.

In the end, accounts can help depersonalize disagreements in negotiation. Accounts move the disagreement from emotions to objective standards. Accounts make the disagreement about what you deserve or what the circumstances warrant. In addition, they center the discussion on a problem that the two of you can work together to solve.

On balance, these three counteroffer tactics—leading with your target, packaging to expand the pie, and justifying your requests—should lead to approaches like the following:

> *"I was looking for a salary in the $70,000 range [leading with my target] because that's what other companies have been offering applicants with my experience and past performance record [justifying my request]. However, since you are unable to go this high, I would be willing to accept a $67,000 salary in exchange for either an additional $3,000 in moving expenses, or a company car [proposing multiple packages to expand the pie]. This package is consistent with what other companies seem to be offering applicants at my level [justifying my request]."*

An approach like this identifies your target, shows your concessions, and accounts for your request.

USING YOUR ALTERNATIVE OFFER

One issue that often arises in the give-and-take exchange of a negotiation is whether you should disclose any other offers you may have in hand. If you have a very strong alternative, disclosing it can frame your concessions even more strongly than leading with your targets. If another employer already has offered you a $68,000 salary, mentioning that offer really drives home the point that your willingness to accept a $65,000 salary is a concession—a *gain* for this employer. It drives home the point more strongly than your target of $70,000 because that other offer is a concrete alternative of yours, not just a wish. Sharing this information also serves to substantiate your current market value and should reassure this employer that the company is (would be) getting its money's worth.

In the early stages of offers and counteroffers, it is important

that your alternatives be presented as evidence of the value you bring and not as a threat. This is a subtle but important distinction. A strong alternative legitimates your worth. On the other hand, an early threat may undermine your attempts to enlist the employer's help in identifying a mutually satisfactory agreement.

Eventually you may sense that you have expanded what there is to expand and claimed what there is to claim. At that point, it will be time to close the deal.

- If you get an "exploding offer"—an offer with a very short fuse—find an alternative (more time, a better offer, an offer elsewhere) that addresses both sides' underlying interests.

- Leading with your targets helps the employer understand your underlying interests and frames any concessions you make for the employer.

- Framing helps the employer see your concessions as gains, which makes the employer more likely to avoid the risk of impasse by accepting your offer.

- Always get something in exchange for concessions you make. The best way to do this is to package concessions you offer as trades for concessions by the employer.

- By proposing several different packages that are good for you, you can expand the pie by letting the employer find the package that offers the company the most value.

- You can use your alternatives in your accounts to help frame your counteroffer to claim more value.

7 SPEED BUMPS AND OTHER DEAL KILLERS

Chris squirmed. This was really making him uncomfortable. "Wasn't a company car part of the package last year?" he asked.

Mr. Burton frowned ever so slightly. "Not exactly. Yes, Sally Jones got a car last year. But that was a special situation. I know that your current employer does not provide company cars for any of its employees. Of course if you have a third offer you have not yet told me about, we would take that into consideration. But for now, we are not offering you a company car."

Chris felt his face flush. He didn't have another offer. But Mr. Burton couldn't know that, could he? What Chris did have was a couple of other interviews elsewhere. But those were just possibilities—that certainly wasn't worth much leverage, was it?

"Well, I am talking with Williams-Gerard," said Chris. "It would only be fair for you to match their offer, wouldn't it?" Chris knew that Mr. Burton might take this to mean that Williams-Gerard had made him an offer. He felt a twinge of guilt, but reminded himself that all people exaggerate when they negotiate. Don't they?

That got Mr. Burton's attention. "Williams-Gerard? Who are you talking with there?"

A moment passed before his Williams-Gerard contact person came to mind. "Jean Thompson," he added quickly. Actually, Chris hadn't even met Thompson yet; that was *next* week. "Why do you ask?"

Mr. Burton gazed out the window for a moment. "Williams-Gerard is a fine company. Of course, we have more regional offices and that means more opportunities for upward mobility. You know, I have an old school friend who works over there."

An old school friend? Now that didn't sound good at all. Chris decided to clear the air on this before he got in too deep. "Right now, it's just a possibility of course. We haven't even really started talking."

"Yes," nodded Mr. Burton, "I know."

Keeping Your Eyes on the Prize

Despite every attempt to conduct a constructive "value-added" approach to negotiation, the process is not always straightforward. There are a few "speed bumps" that negotiators encounter on the road to a satisfying agreement. In this chapter, we address how to deal with these speed bumps and still keep your eyes on the prize, how to recognize and combat attempts by the other side to confuse you, and how to avoid the temptation to confuse things yourself. Although potential deal killers, these speed bumps won't stop you if you're prepared for them.

> ## DEAL BREAKERS
>
> - Emotional Reactions
> - "Fairness Talk"
> - Misrepresentation

Emotional Reactions

For good or for bad, emotional reactions accompany every important moment in our lives. An offer of $60,000 in salary is just such a moment and is sure to include warm feelings like relief and validation. The problem is that many of us have difficulty separating the facts of the offer from the emotional experience that accompanies it.

Emotions can create transitory value in negotiation. They can make issues take on value during a negotiation that those issues didn't have before the negotiation and won't have after it. You may feel a warm rush of relief and validation when you are offered a $60,000 salary, but your salary will still be $60,000 long after that warm rush of relief and validation has vanished.

IDENTIFY THE CURSE

Emotions can contribute to both the **"Winner's Curse"** and the **"Loser's Curse"** in negotiation. The winner's curse occurs when you say "yes" to a deal and regret it later. For example, you say yes to an inferior compensation package for fear that you will lose the job if you don't. Later you regret it when you compare what you got to what you think you should have gotten. Typically, this means you conceded too much to get something you wanted (the job). The loser's curse occurs when you say "no" to a deal and regret it later. You failed to reach agreement—when you really could have had a good deal. For example, you say no to a good offer because you think you should do better. Typically this means you tried to get too much and, as a consequence, ended up with nothing (no job).

Why do the winner's curse and loser's curse occur? Negotiations have a certain momentum, much of which is based on our feelings about how the facts of the negotiation are going. Maybe you feel a need to finish what you have started. Maybe you're afraid to lose what you have already "earned," you don't want to disappoint the other side, or you want them to like you. Maybe the certainty of having an agreement—any agreement—begins to loom large in comparison to the uncertainty of continuing to negotiate. Maybe you desperately want to avoid starting over again with someone else. All of these can lead you to say yes when you really mean no (the winner's curse). Maybe you're afraid to stop trying for more. Maybe you're afraid that you haven't asked for enough, or that you're being taken advantage of. Maybe the employer made you mad and you are more focused on getting even (or winning) than on benefiting yourself. All of these can lead you to continue saying no when you really mean to say yes (the loser's curse).

Emotional responses can reveal legitimate interests that an applicant (or employer!) feels but has not yet articulated. Perhaps starting over elsewhere really isn't worth the additional value you could obtain by doing so. Perhaps you really are being taken advantage of. Perhaps the employer's goodwill really is worth taking a slightly lower offer. **What distinguishes emotions that reflect your real interests from emotions that cloud your view of your truly lasting interests is whether you reach the same conclusion later when you are not immediately involved in the negotiation.** Would you reach the same conclusion if you were advising yourself? If your recommendation as an outside advisor would have been no when you said yes, or yes when you said no, then your decision was a transitory emotional reaction. You are not deciding based on the facts of the negotiation; you are deciding based on your emotional reactions to those facts.

AVOID THE CURSE

Because emotions can reflect transitory value, you need to manage your emotions in negotiation. When emotions represent transitory value, the passage of time can allow them to boil away, to reveal what value is really underneath. Whether you are feeling anger, joy, panic, or elation, feelings are not what negotiation should be about (unless they really *are* what this negotiation is about for you). Typically it is not the feelings that are the prize; it is the value you obtain from the issues that is the prize. It is not feelings you end up with. You end up with the value you negotiate on the issues. So play for time.

A good way to play for time is to ask for the current offer in writing. We suggest that you try not to accept an offer until you have seen it in writing for two reasons.

> ## TRY NOT TO ACCEPT AN OFFER UNTIL YOU SEE IT IN WRITING
>
> - The request will give you the time to think and check the role of your emotions before you make a decision that can determine the rest of your life.
>
> - It is not uncommon for negotiators to *agree* to an offer only to discover later that they actually *disagree* as to the exact terms of that agreement.

A written offer provides you the opportunity to see that your perceptions and the employer's match, and that the employer hasn't forgotten anything you thought he/she had agreed to. If the employer says something isn't important enough to put in writing, point out (in a friendly manner) that if it isn't important they shouldn't mind putting it in writing.

The Fairness Challenge

Fairness is a topic in negotiation that often evokes strong emotions and thus represents a potential speed bump on the road to a satisfactory agreement. **Fairness is about the appropriate standards for dividing up the available value.**

When someone says,

"You are not being fair."

they don't just mean that you are not offering them what they want. They mean that according to some standard, you *should be* offering them more than you are. The idea of standards is key here. **Fairness talk can be used as a tactic in negotiation to convince you that what you have been offered is what you should want, or that you should be offering more in return.** The point of an employer's "fairness challenge" is to get you to see your demands as too high (you are demanding more than what is appropriate) or to see that their offer is a good one (it is as good as you should expect). When an employer says, "Your demands are not fair," the employer wants you to lower your demands; when the employer says, "Our offer is a fair one," the employer wants you to see it as appropriate and accept it. The employer wants you to stop asking for more!

Fairness standards are about the ratio of inputs to outcomes. *Inputs* are what you bring to the job (including your experience, expertise, effort, and performance). *Outcomes* are what the employer gives you in exchange (including salary, job satisfaction, growth on the job, status—anything you receive in exchange for being an employee). When someone says, "Your demands are not fair," they mean that in comparison to the value you demand from them (for example, salary) the value you offer in exchange (for example, your experience) is not appropriate, according to some standard.

Where do fairness standards come from? The appropriate ratio of inputs to outcomes can come from objective measures such as the labor costs necessary to turn a profit. In this case, employee salaries that drive the employer out of business or decrease as profits increase are unfair. It is very difficult to find and agree on the "objective" factors that should be included in fairness calculations. **No applicant is interested in working for subsistence, and no employer is interested in simply breaking even. Both want to do well. But how well is fair?**

Fairness standards also entail comparisons to others. An employer thinks an offer is fair when the ratio of inputs to outcomes is the same as those offered to other applicants. When an employer says, "Our offer is fair," the employer often means you are being offered what similar others have been (or are being) offered. But the question remains, who are the "similar others" to whom you should be compared—other state-university graduates, other sales representatives in Chicago, other applicants hired by the firm, other applicants hired by the firm as sales representatives?

What makes fairness talk in negotiation difficult is that applicants and employers typically do not use the same standards. What looks fair to the applicant may not seem fair to the employer. This conflict happens because applicants and employers use different standards as the basis for comparison.

Fairness only means getting what everyone else gets if you are giving what everyone else gives. If you are going to give more, you should get more—that's only fair. As a new hire, however, a recruiter cannot know with certainty how much you are going to give or how much value you will provide to the firm. Therefore, the employer's tendency when calculating and "talking fairness" is to address the equality of the outcomes offered to similar others and not the inputs. The employer assumes that all new hires will provide the same value. This means a fair offer *from the employer's perspective* is the *same* offer made to similar employees—whoever the employer thinks those similar employees might be!

A fairness challenge works because of uncertainty. No one, neither employer nor applicant, can really know what is fair. Every applicant is completely unique, and that means: (1) the inputs you bring (your experience, education, expertise, effort) are going to be unique, and (2) it is difficult to know which similar others (similar on which of your many individual characteristics) are the right comparison.

A fairness challenge also works because no one wants to think of themselves as unfair or be considered unfair. Fairness talk is meant to remind you that people who want more than similar others are greedy, unreasonable, and ungrateful. Thus, "fairness talk" works because it elicits an emotional response—a fear of being a bad person.

TAKING ON THE FAIRNESS CHALLENGE

FOUR WAYS TO TAKE ON THE FAIRNESS CHALLENGE

- Ask pointed questions to uncover the "why" (interests and standards) behind the challenge.

- Change the employer's perception of the value of what you bring to the table (change the inputs).

- Change the employer's perception of the value of the offer to you (change the outcomes).

- Change those the employer uses for comparison (change the similar others).

We recommend that you respond to a fairness challenge by asking pointed questions to uncover the "why" behind the challenge. For example, you might ask:

> *"What leads you to believe that my demands are unfair? What is your offer based on? What would be fair? Why?"*

Questions like these will help you uncover the "why" (interests and standards) behind the employer's fairness challenge. If you don't understand the "why," you can't take on the challenge. If you don't take on the challenge, you won't change the employer's mind.

Once you know what the other side's standards are for *fairness*, you have three effective ways to take on the challenge:

THREE WAYS TO TAKE ON THE FAIRNESS CHALLENGE

- Change the employer's perception of the *input* you bring.

- Change the *outcome* the employer offers.

- Change the *similar others* the employer uses for comparison.

Your Input. **You can use the employer's own standards of fairness to get what you want by pointing out how or why the input you offer exceeds that of similar employees.** Make a case for how the value you bring (your education, experience, expertise,

111

and effort) will increase the company's outcome. Focus on the unique value you bring and how the organization will benefit from this unique value. If the employer is not convinced, find a way to guarantee the return on the employer's investment as promised. This will reduce the employer's risk and ensure that the agreement you propose will fulfill the employer's standard of fairness.

You might propose a "contingency contract" that makes your outcome contingent on your input. For example, an applicant could propose a salary contingent on actual performance. The applicant receives the employer's salary offer if the applicant's performance only meets the employer's expectations. However, if the applicant **exceeds** the employer's performance expectations, the salary offer will be increased by some percentage proposed by the applicant. A contingency contract decreases both your risk and that of the employer.

Your Outcome. **A second approach is to change the employer's assessment of your outcome.** Two anchors will allow you to do this. The first anchor is an alternative offer. **If you have an attractive alternative, you can point out that the compensation (outcome) you can get elsewhere is greater than this employer has offered you.** If the employer tries to bait you by suggesting that you seem too focused on compensation and not enough on the opportunity, remind the employer:

"I recognize and appreciate the great opportunity that this position offers. But I also have to be concerned about compensation. Salary and compensation records serve as a signal to the industry regarding my value, and I cannot afford to produce the wrong

signal. By definition, a great opportunity means a great oppor-tunity to bring value to your organization, and I am simply ask-ing to be compensated for that value."

A second anchor to use is your current salary *plus* additional compensation for your willingness to make a change. **Remind the employer that you (and your family) will incur consider-able transaction costs if you accept the offer.** Consequently, the total compensation must justify the costs of the move. On average, you should expect a new offer to exceed your current compensation package by 10 to 15 percent. Remember, how-ever, that only you can decide what increase is sufficient. Your old salary is likely to serve as a benchmark for the new offer. This can be costly if your old salary was far below the market. Remember, what you are offered is not necessarily what you can obtain.

The "Similar Others." The third tactic is to change the "similar others" to whom you are being compared. Imagine that the salary you are offered is consistent with the mean salary being paid for the same position in the current market. **Remind the employer that the organization is interested in you pre-cisely because you will bring significantly more to the organ-ization than the average new hire. Consequently, your com-pensation should be commensurate with offers at the *top* of the market—not the average!** If the average new hire is being offered $60,000, you should get more than $60,000 if you bring more experience or more expertise to the table or have a record of greater effort, commitment, and success.

Imagine that the employer tells you that your offer reflects your relative lack of experience or limited training. How should you respond? What population can you use to reanchor the discussion? We suggest that you explain how uncomfortable you would be to receive less compensation than other new hires and current employees.

"If I receive less than other new hires and current employees I am starting at a disadvantage that will be difficult to overcome. A lower compensation level will send a negative signal to coworkers regarding my competency. You must feel that I have sufficient value to contribute or you would not have made me an offer. I would be willing to accept a contingency contract that compensates me at the same level as everyone else—until my performance suggests I don't deserve it.

Again, this approach attempts to change whom you are compared to and reduces the risk to the employer. When considering which avenue to use to address the employer's fairness concerns, remember that these concerns generally stem from a need for internal equity (the employer doesn't want to slight current employees), organizational equity (the employer wants to receive sufficient "bang in return for their buck"), and applicant equity (you want to feel you are justly compensated for your effort). Therefore, choose an anchor that aggressively supports your case and addresses the fairness concerns of the employer.

In the final analysis, the only "fair" offer is one that appeases both sides. You can deal with a fairness challenge effectively by understanding the other side's underlying interests—including their concerns about fairness—and addressing them. It is okay to want what you want, even if concerns about fairness are not what motivate what you want. However, you are more likely to get what you want if you can address or shift the other side's standards and address their fairness concerns.

Misrepresentation

Information is obviously a key resource in negotiation. After all, information provides the foundation for expanding the pie and claiming value. It is not surprising, then, that misrepresentation is sometimes a problem in negotiation. An applicant may claim something is important that is not, while an employer may claim something is impossible that can be done. In either case, one side is trying to mislead the other by misrepresenting their underlying interests.

Typically misrepresentation takes one of three forms:

THE THREE FORMS OF MISREPRESENTATION

■ Saying you must have something that you can live without

■ Saying you have been offered something that you have not been offered

■ Saying you do not care about something that you do care about

Each of these tactics creates problems. Let's deal with each type of misrepresentation in turn.

"I Must Have Something." Applicants sometimes say they must have something that they can live without. Using this tactic implies that you may turn down the offer if the recruiter does not cave in and meet your demands. This is a very dangerous game. If it is in the employer's power to grant a strong preference, there are better ways to get it granted than to use threats. If the employer is unable to do so, a threat will not work.

If your threat is a bluff and your bluff is called, you have two choices:

YOUR CHOICES WHEN THEY CALL YOUR BLUFF

■ You can follow through on your threat and walk away from this offer (not a good choice!).

■ You can admit that you were bluffing (an even worse choice!).

You can keep the offer or your reputation but not both. The only person you back into a corner with a threat is yourself. So be well advised. Only draw a line in the sand if you are prepared to have them cross it.

Even if your bluff is not called, exaggerating the strength of your preference may cost you elsewhere. Remember, there is no such thing as a free lunch. The recruiter only has so much total value to give you. Getting more in one area may require the employer to give you less in another. So wish for what you want, but be careful what you demand.

"I've Been Offered It Elsewhere." The most common form of misrepresentation is to misrepresent your alternatives. You do that when you misrepresent your current salary or say that you have received an alternative offer that you have not. Only you can decide what tactics to use, but we strongly discourage this practice. Instead, we encourage you to conduct yourself in the most professional and straightforward manner possible. **Only make statements or quote figures that you can justify.** It is not uncommon for employers to try to verify the information you give them. Your reputation and credibility take a lifetime to develop but only a moment to destroy.

"That's Not Important." Applicants are often reluctant to tell employers what they want for fear the employer will hold it hostage and demand something in return. For example, an applicant who wants a particular location may misrepresent this preference for fear that the employer will use this information strategically and withhold the location until the applicant accepts a lower salary. To avoid this, an applicant may pretend not to care which office location he is assigned to.

Unfortunately, this tactic can backfire. You may have to explain later why you are not willing to make concessions on an issue you claimed was unimportant or why you suddenly don't want a settlement option that you previously claimed to prefer. **The interests you represent to the other side are the only interests the other side can address.** If you want the other side to give you what you want, you will need to be truthful about what you want.

There may be situations where misrepresentations can (apparently) give you leverage. Some negotiators believe it is okay to misrepresent information if they never expect to deal with the other side again or there is no way for the other side to find out. So what is the right answer? Should you misrepresent?

In the final analysis, it is not the role of this book to take a moral stance on misrepresentation. It is the role of this book to provide you sound practical advice. So here it is. You should consider the costs, and you should consider the alternatives. The costs are not trivial. If nothing else, **your credibility and self-respect are two of the most valuable assets you possess.** In addition, this book gives you plenty of better alternatives for getting what you want. Often the only way to get information is to give it. **Information exchange should always be a reciprocal process.** If you are going to provide information about your interests, you should (at the very least) always receive an equivalent amount of information about the other side's interests in exchange.

Some Conclusions on Speed Bumps

Don't ever forget that the goal of negotiation is to claim as much value as you can for yourself. And don't ever forget that is the employer's goal as well. Employers will try to make a good deal for themselves and for their company. You need to keep your eyes on the prize—the value you want to claim in this negotiation exchange. "Fairness talk" is a way to confuse you, and misrepresentation is a way to confuse them. Emotions confuse everyone. All of these minor speed bumps can become substantial detours. These distractions make it easy for both sides to fall back on their "fixed-pie" tendencies, particularly when the going gets tough. The better you can manage these speed bumps, the better you are able to maintain a focus on both sides' underlying interests. Handle them effectively and you can be well on your way to closing the deal!

- Keeping your eyes on the prize means maintaining a focus on both sides' underlying interests and your goal in negotiation.

- Negotiations have momentum that can be tied up in emotions. Emotions can contribute to both the "Winner's Curse" (saying yes to the deal you don't want) and the "Loser's Curse" (saying no to a deal you do want).

- When emotions take over, take a break and reconvene when emotions have subsided.

- "Fairness talk" is a tactic for claiming value. Fairness talk is about the comparison between the value you bring to the company and the value it offers you. To deal with a fairness challenge, find out what *standards* the other side is using. Then change the employer's perception of your input, your outcome, or the appropriate "others" he/she compares to you.

- When you misrepresent your interests, you mislead the other side. This has costs in both the short run and the long run.

8 Closing the Deal

Chris scanned the offer one more time. He knew that he was being compulsive, but he wanted to be sure that he had not missed anything. He looked up as Mr. Burton came back into the office.

"So, Chris, does the revised contract cover what we discussed?" Mr. Burton asked as he leaned back in his chair.

"I think so. It looks like I will get an initial salary of $55,000 but will receive an additional $5,000 in base pay contingent on my completing the six-month training program in the upper half of the class. Is that correct?"

"Yes."

"Great. In addition, you will cover 50 percent of my moving expenses and pay off what I still owe in student financial aid."

"That is correct. We know that these initial investments in you along with the $6,000 signing bonus will greatly relieve your financial burden and allow you to focus on the training program and what you can contribute in Chicago. You bring a nice skill set to the Marketing Department that we want to capitalize on from day one," Mr. Burton said with a smile.

"I really appreciate the effort you invested in trying to make this work. I know you went to bat for me and I will not forget it. Thanks again. I want you to know that all of these issues plus the three weeks of vacation time have enhanced my commitment and determination to make the most out of this remarkable opportunity. I believe we have a deal, Mr. Burton," Chris said, as he reached across the table to give Mr. Burton a firm handshake.

"Welcome on board, Chris. Let's go celebrate!" Mr. Burton said, as he came around the desk to pat Chris on the back.

If you do manage to keep your eyes on the prize and avoid potential speed bumps, you'll be well on your way to an agreement. The more likely possibility, however, is that some final "move" will be necessary to close the deal. There are two places to look for that final move: *extending the time horizon* and *talking walk away*.

Extending the Time Horizon

Extending the time horizon means making concessions today for promised compensation tomorrow. This technique is a pie-expanding approach to closing that final gap between what you want and what the other side is offering. To this point in the book, we have focused on immediate, present forms of value in negotiation. However, trades that help both sides are not limited to the present. Extending the time horizon to include future benefits is another way to expand the pie.

THE "INSTALLMENT PLAN"

A simple way to extend the time horizon is to accept value "on the installment plan." When you get compensation on the installment plan, you get some now and some later. An example of accepting value on the installment plan would be agreeing to a lower salary, but with a guaranteed minimum salary increase for next year.

The installment plan is a good tactic if the employer doesn't have any more value to give you right now. Imagine that you and your employer are still $3,000 apart in salary, and the negotiation has bogged down. If the employer can't budge because there isn't any more salary money in the budget this year, perhaps there would be enough money in the budget next year or the year after. By agreeing to the offered salary and a $5,000 guaranteed minimum increase above the usual merit-pay increase in years two and three, you can make it possible for the employer to give you more value.

CONTINGENT COMPENSATION

Another way to extend the time horizon is through performance-contingent compensation or "pay for performance." What often creates that final gap between what the employer is willing to offer and what the applicant wants is a difference in each side's beliefs about the applicant's probable performance: the value that the employer will receive in return for compensation provided. If both sides knew exactly what the applicant was worth, this would not be a problem. However, there is always some uncertainty. Employers don't want to overpay, while applicants don't want to undersell themselves. Furthermore, applicants are likely to be overconfident about their abilities and probable accomplishments. This means that applicants are likely to think they are worth more than employers are willing to pay.

Performance-contingent compensation is a way to bridge this gap between employer's and applicant's beliefs about the applicant's probable performance. Compensation is provided at a level contingent on performance. The better the applicant performs, the more compensation he/she receives. Sales commissions, piecework pay, and performance bonuses are all examples of performance-contingent compensation.

Performance-contingent compensation can reduce the risk of uncertainty for both sides. The applicant knows that he/she will be paid commensurate with his/her performance; the employer knows that the company will pay only for performance achieved. Both sides agree that the compensation will be appropriate, even while they disagree about what the eventual performance and subsequent compensation will be.

GET IT IN WRITING

Because extended time-horizon agreements promise future compensation for future performance, they are important to get in writing. People and circumstances change in organizations. The person you negotiate with may leave the company before you ever get a chance to claim the promised future compensation. It is not uncommon, for example, for students in the midst of a company-funded M.B.A. program to find that their newly acquired company will no longer pay their tuition. It can be easy for unwritten obligations to become forgotten, so get them in writing.

"TALKING WALK AWAY"

Extending the time horizon expands the pie by including future considerations (perhaps even contingent ones) in the total value each side receives. In contrast, talking walk away is a value-claiming way to try to close that final gap between applicant and employer. Talking walk away means threatening to end the negotiation and accept an impasse.

Why would you walk away from a negotiation? You should walk away if you have an alternative that offers you more value. Getting an agreement is not always the right outcome. **If the other side will not or cannot give you what you want, need, or deserve, you should walk away.**

If you reach the point of walk away, it is critical to be honest with yourself and ask some important questions. Are you sure that there aren't other issues through which you could recoup the missing value? Are you sure that your demands and expectations are realistic? Remember, you don't want to walk away from what is actually a good deal—that's the loser's curse. If your answer to both questions is yes, it is appropriate to walk away (to avoid the winner's curse).

Remember that walking away doesn't get you what you want. Getting the other side to agree to what you want gets you what you want. **Always give the other side a chance to play their final card. If something in the offer is a "deal breaker," explain this to the other side before you walk away.** This gives the other side a last opportunity to make things work. Let the employer know what it would take for you to say yes and then leave it to the employer to say yes or no.

Some Conclusions on Conclusions

Keeping your attention focused on underlying interests is necessary to successfully close a deal, but it may not be sufficient. To close the final gap between employer offer and applicant aspirations may require that you extend the time horizon of the negotiation—**use the promise of the future to expand the pie in the present.** As a last resort, closing that gap may even require talking walk away. However, if it comes to this, always remember that talking walk away works best when it accomplishes what extending the time horizon accomplishes—getting the other side to give you what you want.

- "Extending the time horizon" and "talking walk away" are two ways to close that final gap between employer offer and applicant aspirations.

- Getting compensation "on the installment plan" simply means the promise of additional compensation in the future. The installment plan is a good tactic if the employer has no more value to offer you in the present.

- Performance-contingent compensation bridges the gap between the employer's and applicant's beliefs about the applicant's probable performance. The better the applicant performs, the more compensation the applicant will receive.

- "Talking walk away" means threatening to end the negotiation. Always give the other side a chance to play their final card before you walk away. Tell them what the offer has to be for you to say yes and then let them say yes or no to your final request.

9 Tales from the Hiring Line: Lessons Learned from Job Applicants and Employers

About Our Panel of Experts

We have spent the last fifteen years helping people like you improve your ability to negotiate effectively. During this time, we have learned a great deal from both practice and research. This chapter allows us to share many of the questions, answers, warnings, ideas, and insights so many people have shared with us. When coupled with your own experiences, this dialogue should bring to life many of the concepts introduced in this book. We know that you will benefit as much from the dialogue among our panel of applicants, employers, recruiters, headhunters and scholars as we have.

POINT-COUNTER-POINT

After surveying hundreds of applicants, we compiled a list of the most commonly asked questions and pressing concerns. We then asked a distinguished panel of employment professionals (including corporate recruiters, human resource executives, outplacement personnel, and career services professionals) to address these questions and concerns.

What follows is an eclectic mix of insights derived from the varied experiences of our panel members given their different roles, functions, and industries. While each answer is interesting and informative in its own right, the most significant lessons can be derived from the overall pattern of responses. Read each of the questions posed by the candidates and consider what your own answer might be before reading the answers provided by us and our panel.

PANEL OF EMPLOYMENT PROFESSIONALS*

A. Sarah V. Hey of AIDE, Inc.

B. Tom Fowler of The Hindman Company

C. Mike McMillin of tmp.worldwide

D. Thomas Fernandez of Columbia University

E. Greg Satterwhite of Federal Express

F. Laura Littlejohn of Pritchett & Associates Inc.

G. Lori Albert of CMS

H. Rick L. Miller of IBM

I. Steven Lubrana of Dartmouth University

J. Elizabeth Duncklee of University of Chicago

K. Barry Pryer of Sewell Lexus

L. Wesley Millican of Ray & Berndtson, Inc.

*Letters preceding panel members correspond to the responses in this chapter.

Common Applicant Questions and Panel Answers

QUESTION 1

I have just received an offer from a Big-Six accounting firm and was informed that the salary was nonnegotiable because all new trainees receive the same salary. Should I attempt to negotiate in "nonnegotiable" situations such as this when the employer seems to have a take-it-or-leave-it attitude?

RESPONSES

A. Yes, but have something in writing to back up what you are worth in the marketplace for your skill set.

D. Rarely is nothing negotiable, so always negotiate.

F. Determine the profile of the average trainee at this firm. I doubt if everyone truly does receive the same package, given diversity in education, work experience, leadership skills, etc. If this person is above average, the firm should be willing to pay top dollar to increase their own average standards.

H. No matter what they tell you, salaries are always negotiable. However, negotiating with the recruiter may not be the best method. He/she is the gatekeeper. Their responsibility is to hire the best candidate for the least amount of money. A better tactic is to try negotiating with the person that you will be working for, being tactful in your approach.

I.   Parity at the early level is critical with a big class of equally qualified individuals. Performance will identify stars, and compensation will follow in subsequent years.

J.   Present objective evidence in a polite manner. The candidate should note that if he/she is outside of the profile of the typical candidate for the position, he/she should not expect to command the salary the typical candidate receives.

L.   One should always negotiate as long as there exists the ability to illustrate through the use of decision anchors (i.e., industry standards, personal accomplishments, etc.), the added current and/or future value that one will bring to the institution in question. Representing your worth in this manner will keep the negotiations at a value-added level and will reduce the perceived risk incurred by your employer by approving the additional compensation. One might choose to utilize the above technique in addressing financial concerns with those to whom you will report, as future bosses can be key advocates in compensation hiring matters. Additionally, one should question requesting additional compensation if support anchors for such a request cannot be substantiated. It can leave negative impressions with your employer as to your character and motivations where the company is concerned. Finally, one should consider the negotiation style of the company representative(s) and understand that it will tend to reflect the management style(s) currently utilized within the company.

Authors. Begin with a question such as "why is this your policy?" Remember that addressing an issue *before* you really know what motivates it is like shooting an arrow without knowing the target. Once you know what the problem is, try to obtain additional value in a way that avoids the problem.

The strategies available to you include changing their perception of your input, outcome, or comparison to others (if, for example, they feel they cannot distinguish among new applicants), contracts (if they feel the proof is in the pudding), or finding issues that are less restricted, such as a signing bonus, stock options, tuition reimbursement, or early performance review (if they are just concerned about following the mandates of the policy).

Question 2

What should you do if an employer has a set benefit package or has offered you an unacceptable package?

Responses

B. An individual won't be able to change a company's benefit plan, but remember that some benefits may outweigh others. There may be some benefits you haven't thought about going into but that are worth as much. Look at everything. Know and understand the package before evaluating it. If you want a 401K but they only have a pension plan, consider it because it may be worth as much or more.

D. If you are very interested in the firm, explain your problem.

F. I had a personal experience where a firm I was very interested in clearly had much different salary ideas than I did. After saying the company would like to offer me a job, the recruiter asked me what my salary expectations were so he could take this back to the department where I would be working. Not wanting to throw the first number and not knowing their range at this point, I expressed openness on this subject and offered public statistics from the career center on consulting salaries from the previous year. His reaction was of great surprise and concern, as the company had intended a considerably lower offer.

Although I liked a number of things about this firm, I was also interviewing with a couple of other companies and had a considerably higher offer holding. After a few days of going back and forth, I was told that this firm simply couldn't meet this. We had a very open conversation about all this. I gave the recruiter my bottom line, and the company couldn't meet it. I was prepared to walk away, which I did. Luckily, I could afford to, although I was disappointed. After a short time, the company contacted me again and we brainstormed about how they could provide the value I was originally seeking in salary in some other form of compensation. We came up with a larger signing bonus, some profit-sharing, and an earlier performance review. This tactic wouldn't have worked if I hadn't had another offer; it would have looked terrible to make that stand then come crawling back.

H. One could compare it to other industry packages in the negotiation to demonstrate the weakness in the offering. This minimizes the emotional issues and maximizes the sense of fairness.

I. I would not expect them to shake the foundation for an individual. They would be crazy to do so. I would suggest they generate market data points for comparison and offer to help them with the effort. If you cannot increase the package and it is not acceptable, look for another job. Recognize the tight market, take what you can get, and then change from within.

J. I would advise the candidate to look for other ways to "make the package whole." In other words, perhaps try to negotiate more salary or bonus to make up for the perceived lack presented by the benefit package.

L. A *set benefits package* is not something a company can feasibly or legally change to meet the needs of each individual hired. Before considering a negotiation strategy, one should ascertain the true net values and risks involved with both the company's current and offered packages. Companies understand that these conflicts are imminent, as no two companies' benefit packages are identical. Utilize the net value of other mechanisms (i.e., salary, bonuses, stock, vacation days, etc.) as a means to bring "wholeness" to your situation. Your current benefits and/or those in other offers being considered should serve as a major source of leverage. Additionally, one should not forget to point out one's accomplishments and value-added potential against other candidates and market standards.

Authors. Our response to question 1 fits here as well. In fact, our book provides a comprehensive answer to this question. The general steps, however, are as follows:

1. Preparation is key. Be sure you distinguish between an unacceptable package (one that provides value *below* your bottom line) and an undesirable package (one that provides value *above* your bottom line but well below your target).

2. Ask questions to determine specifically what the boundaries, rules, and limitations are and what motivates them.

3. Address the motivation behind the rules not the rules themselves.

4. Look for ways to create value for the employer and his/her organization in such a way that you increase the benefits and curb the costs/risks of having the employer do what you ask.

5. Don't be afraid to walk away.

QUESTION 3

What kind of leverage do you have when it is obvious that you are unemployed or underemployed (due to a small versus large company, industry differences, etc.)? How can you deal with this issue during the negotiation to ensure that you get a salary commensurate with the current market?

RESPONSES

A. Have written verifiable proof of market salaries for your skill set.

B. Make an effort to show that you can fill their needs. That is the issue—not that you are underemployed.

D. Leverage is not the important thing. Candidates have to do research and find out the going salary for that industry, that function, and that firm. After receiving the offer, if necessary, insist that the firm explain why they are not paying you the going rate.

G. Research! Know the market; let the employer know you know the market. Why are you underemployed? Did you take the job because you would gain a valuable skill or because it was the only job you could get? You have some leverage if you can show that you took the job to obtain a skill you did not have or were hired on as an expert to help clean things up. If you have been a valuable asset (i.e., saved the company money, implemented a new computer system that increased productivity, etc.), you will have plenty of leverage. If you are unemployed for a good reason, you should not have lost any leverage. You will still be in demand. If you have been fired, depending on the circumstances, being demanding is not going to be looked upon favorably. Generally, if you are a quality-minded, hard-working, bright candidate, you will be in demand and have some room to negotiate. Been justifiably fired for work that is substandard? If not in demand, take what you can get and work on building your reputation back up. Desperation is not difficult to read and can be used against you.

H. Focus on skills that you have that are transportable across industries. Demonstrate through examples how those skills equal or exceed current market requirements or standards. Then ask to be compensated equally.

I. Take the bull by the horns and show them what you are worth. Unemployed does not have the same stigma of failure it once had—unemployed means "available and interested."

J. Always present objective data to justify your request. No reasonable company will want to pay you less than the going market rate, because you will leave.

L. Employers in these situations are banking on your potential. I have always recommended that people keep a "HERO" file. An acronym for "Helping to Enthusiastically Represent Ourselves," this file contains representative documentation of personal and professional accomplishments and achievements over one's career. This information, when coupled with strong industry knowledge, will provide significant leverage and credibility as you negotiate your value and ability.

Authors. Preparation is the key!!! Be knowledgeable about the marketplace, the position, and your value. Don't be afraid to educate the employer about all of these issues. Attempt to focus the negotiation on the value you bring (remind them that you are preaching to the choir, given that they made you an offer) and not on the existence of your alternatives. Be open about the fact that you are currently unemployed or underemployed and the reasons behind it.

Make it clear, however, that you expect their offer to reflect your *future* value to this organization and NOT your *current* situation. It is very important to move the anchor away from your poor existing alternative (poor compensation or no compensation). If your situation continues to be an issue, remind them that the sooner you reach an agreement, the less likely they are to lose you due to a competitive offer. Your situation is short-term not long-term.

QUESTION 4

My last job change was out of the defense industry, which is much maligned as being full of deadwood and underachievers. How can I deal with this issue?

RESPONSES

B. The defense industry is changing. Deadwood is getting out, and it's survival of the fittest.

C. You could argue that this is the reason that you are transitioning out of that industry. However, if you have been in that industry for very long, you will need to explain why it took you so long to do something about it.

D. The process of getting in the clear and succeeding in the interview process is the same regardless of previous employment. Brush up on interview skills and give clear, specific, quantifiable examples of your success.

G. If you have made a name for yourself at your current company, your reputation can speak volumes. Even companies full of deadwood have stars.

H. You could say you left the industry because you need a bigger challenge and hope that the current employer can provide that needed challenge and new opportunities for you to excel and add value to the organization.

J. In interviews, stress what you have accomplished. Make sure that your responses are quantified, if possible, to help drive home your results.

Authors. Deal candidly with this possible perception without making disparaging remarks about your current organization and coworkers. The way you talk about current situations will say something about how you are likely to talk about your future situation. You can point out that some of your skills and interests are currently underutilized, which motivates your decision to seek a new challenge. Focus on those skills, as well as what you've learned from your current situation that will allow you to motivate, challenge, and inspire your future peers and those who report to you.

QUESTION 5

Can a company obtain my past salary history when I have neither provided this information nor given my consent?

RESPONSES

B. They may ask to get a copy of your W2. This is important information for employers. If they sense you are not being truthful, they won't be comfortable about you. It is very dangerous ground to inflate salary information.

D. Lots of information is available; assume you have no privacy. Salary history is irrelevant—compensation should be based on the going rate for the job.

E. Not to my knowledge, legally anyway.

F. HR departments should not share this, but the companies will certainly pressure you for the information! I hated this (when interviewing for jobs out of my M.B.A. program) because my pre-graduate-school salary was considerably lower than my expectations for postschool jobs. People would always ask, but I didn't want them to consider that any type of gauge for what to offer me now. Whenever possible, I went around the issue, but a couple of times was pressured into the conversation. I had completed my M.B.A. degree and had additional work experience (with internships). If I had been satisfied with the level I was at then, I wouldn't have gone back to school to improve my abilities and skills. Given my accomplishments, my current value is now . . ."

G. Yes, probably. Is it ethical? Probably not.

H. No, not with a company I have ever worked with.

L. In this world of information technology and networking, one should assume that anything is discoverable and should never make a compensation-package request based on false assumptions. This can severely damage one's credibility and have a long-lasting impact on one's career. On the other hand, you should take the time to know the true net value of your current financial arrangement so as to avoid leaving any leverage and eventual compensation on the table. Be sure, however, that you are able to clearly articulate your value assessment, as misunderstandings on this issue can have the same negative effect as a true misrepresentation.

Authors. This information should be protected unless you work for a governmental agency or fall into another category that requires your salary title to be published for public consumption. However, don't underestimate how small a world we live in or how much access motivated people can have to otherwise private information.

Much can be done to shift the focus of the negotiator away from the anchor of your salary history if they do obtain it. When the talk is about your salary, tell him/her that you are looking for a future salary consistent with the current market, your education, recent projects, patterns of success, or alternative offers. Worry less about whether they can obtain this information and more about how you can strategically anchor the discussion whether they have the information or not.

QUESTION 6

Should you negotiate a severance package and, if so, how?

B. In general, it is a negative impression up front that you lack confidence. However, there are cases where it makes sense. Example: A company hires a VP of engineering who is fifty-eight years old. The company is up for sale and he is afraid he will lose his job if the new company is downsized. The old management wants to assure him he will be able to stay; the individual wants to be assured that he won't be downsized. It's a win/win situation.

D. Not when you interview or before being terminated. When terminated, say nothing and agree to nothing at first. Take time to think about what you want and need, then present your proposal. Firms do not want trouble and are likely to acquiesce.

G. Only in two conditions: (1) you are top dog, and (2) your industry is volatile. In either case, protect yourself in case of a buyout, shift in management, etc.

L. The appropriateness of negotiating a severance package is held in the eye of the beholder. The motivations for doing so should be well thought-out so as to avoid any negative connotations regarding your character or future intentions. The decision to negotiate a severance package should be a situational response to your current professional and employment status. If you are currently a senior executive and/or you are being heavily recruited, the negotiation of a severance package can be an appropriate mechanism for reducing the uncertainty of your future employment, but more important, reducing the risk incurred by leaving your current position. Be careful, though, as severance packages may contain restrictive covenants relating to position and/or industry and can create situations of reduced employment and compensation freedom in the future. The value of this impact should be figured into severance considerations.

*Authors.*Unless you are negotiating a very senior position or a very risky position, we do not recommend that you negotiate severance pay. The costs associated with asking for an escape clause before you have anything to escape outweigh the benefits of risk reduction. Severance can be negotiated later when and if you need it.

QUESTION 7

What signs should I look for when deciding whether to push or to stop?

RESPONSES

B. When they get defensive or they act like you are treating them unfairly, you've gone too far *for the moment*—but not necessarily too far.

C. When the employer says that this is the final offer, I think that I would stop.

G. It is hard to know. If you are working with a good recruiter, he/she should tell you when you are running out
of room.

H. Tact is very important. Never let the negotiation become
an emotional situation. If it does become emotional,
take a time-out. Return to the negotiation and con-
centrate on fact-based positions—things like skills,
desired characteristics, past achievements, and market
statistics. If the negotiation cannot be centered on fact-
based issues or no longer feels constructive, stop the
negotiation and make a decision on the offer on the
table.

J. Listen to the voice of the person. If it sounds exasper-
ated or strained, stop.

K. There is a time to try it. If it's right, they will let you
push. If not, you will know it and then STOP.

L. If you are noticing signs of emotion and/or defensiveness in your negotiation it may be too late. Key though
invalid perceptions may have already been formed by
the other party and assuredly passed onto others in the
organization. To reduce the risk of such an occurrence,
you should avoid emotion, make sustainable requests
that point out the benefits and reduced risk to the employer, and limit the number of times you go "back to
the well."

Author. Don't base the decision to push or stop on the body language, facial expressions, tone, or emotion of the other party.

Although this sounds counterintuitive, we make this suggestion because:

1. Basing your action on the actions of the other side will allow them to manipulate you.

2. Body language and facial expressions vary in accordance with individual personality, cultural background, gender, and other variables that have nothing to do with what the individual is thinking. If the eyes are the window to the soul, it is an opaque window indeed.

3. Even if body language, facial expression, and tone were accurate measures of thought, most of us are very poor judges of what they mean. We are as likely to misinterpret them as we are to interpret them correctly. This means that we will stop when we could continue and continue when we should stop.

4. When we focus on nonverbal cues, we are not focused on what is being said and withheld. As a consequence we won't have the information that should tell us whether to continue or not. Nor will we have the information we need if we do continue.

So the question remains. What *should* you look for to guide your decision to push or shop? If you have done your job well, you should not have to look at all. If you do your homework enough to be clear about what you want, ask good questions about the specifics of the offer before countering, and provide effective anchors and accounts, the negotiations should feel more like joint problem solving, repeated rounds of bids and counterbids. As a result, you should both know when you have found an agreement that works.

QUESTION 8

If you receive a better offer from another company after accepting a job, should you attempt to renegotiate with this company?

RESPONSES

A. No. Companies can and will rescind the original offer altogether. Most companies do not like to play games—it can lead to a very bad first impression and expectation for when you start the job.

B. No, the game is over. You may want to make the information known so they know they got a good deal and may act favorably in a future review.

C. You can accept the second offer, but by attempting to renegotiate your first offer you raise a red flag as to what your true motivation for being there is. You might let them know that you received another offer, but don't try to renegotiate because of that.

D. Absolutely not. If you accepted a job, you will have to wait until the appropriate time to ask for a raise, probably at performance review time.

G. Which job do you want? Money should never be the deciding factor in any employment situation. If it is, you have not found the right position. If you appear as if you are going after any position that offers more money, a company will question your loyalty.

H. A very dangerous situation. Your acceptance of the job puts your credibility on the line. I would probably mention the offer to see if they would match it. If they didn't, I would honor my original acceptance. I would use the second offer as leverage when it came time for my first salary review.

I. Treat them the way you expect to be treated—you would not want them to lower your salary if some hotshot came in and offered candidacy at a lower entry price. Early negotiators benefit from securing a job—you cannot have your cake and eat it too.

J. NEVER renege on an offer.

L. Attempting to renegotiate a signed deal can negatively impact perceptions about your character and commitment to the organization, both of which will be key to future compensation negotiations and annual reviews. You might, after discussing your commitment to the organization, mention the offer as an anchor for future talks. The other option is to resign and accept the other position but do so because it is a comprehensively better offer. The money, unless significantly different, will mean far less once you go to work. Professional satisfaction must be balanced against financial measures.

Authors. Absolutely not. Your reputation is more valuable than *any* job. Actually, you won't find yourself in this position if you have communicated all of your options as the process proceeds. Before you accept an offer, you should determine which alternatives are still viable and incorporate this information in the negotiation and your decision to accept the offer. Once accepted, you should contact your alternatives to withdraw your candidacy.

QUESTION 9

What kind of leverage can you use with a current employer when trying to get a salary increase or added compensation other than threatening to quit?

RESPONSES

B. A large company may have other opportunities within the company. You may mention to your boss that you would like to be considered for other opportunities. This is not disloyal. A good manager should try to find ways to increase your compensation or find something better for you within the company.

C. How about a track record of outstanding performance? If you do threaten to quit, be ready to follow through with it . . . and remember, if you quit, your employer is not obligated to pay you a severance package.

F. If you have received an offer or have been approached by competitors, share this information so as to show your loyalty, show that you are highly sought after.

G. What have you done for the company? Come armed with your accomplishments and a positive attitude, willing to negotiate.

J. Present your case objectively and logically. Be willing to think of substitutes (e.g., time off with pay instead of an increase in salary or perhaps working four-day weeks instead of five for the same money) that you would be willing to accept.

K. Everyone is worth what the market is willing to pay. Test the market and find out what you can get and then present that tactfully. Never base your argument on need but on worth.

L. All the leverage in the world will not matter if your employer's financial and performance status is not advantageous to such discussions. You must take this into consideration when planning negotiation strategy. Assuming a conducive environment, you must begin with the end in mind and determine how your actions and manner of requests might affect your relationships and peer perceptions once negotiations are completed. As for leverage, comparisons to current market standards, acknowledgement of past performance and contributions, and the ability to reduce the perceived risk to your employer are key. For example: "In return for this increased compensation, I am committed to bringing enhanced effort and results. If I am unable to do so, we can discuss a reduction of my compensation."

Authors. Employers and their organizations vary in terms of how they respond to alternative offers when used as leverage. Some view it favorably (it confirms your value) while others react very negatively (it is a sign of disloyalty and a lack of commitment on your part). Do your homework to determine which type you are dealing with.

If they tend to react favorably, you can go on the market to generate an alternative offer. Do so, however, only if you are willing to seriously consider alternatives. It is unprofessional and disrespectful to ask others to expend the considerable time and resources required during the recruiting process if you have no intention of leaving your current position. If having done so, you find an alternative that your current employer cannot compete with, congratulations! Do not renegotiate with your current employer unless you would consider staying.

Having obtained an alternative, you can approach your current employer following these steps:

1. Inform them about the alternative.

2. Let them know that your preference is to stay if they are willing to reevaluate your current contract.

3. Let them know what you would like (use anchors and accounts) and that you will stay if you get it. (Do not threaten to leave if you fail to get it unless you mean it).

4. Tell them what they can expect to get in return for your improved compensation. Don't ask for something in return for nothing (beyond keeping you). Remember, you always want to increase the value to them of doing what you want.

If they tend to react negatively, we propose a different approach:

1. Tell them that you feel your current compensation no longer reflects your market value or value to the organization (only make this argument if you can provide clear justification).

2. Inform them that you choose not to go on the market because you remain committed to the organization.

3. You hope and trust, however, that they will reconsider your current compensation anyway.

4. Then (again) tell them what they can expect to get in return for your improved compensation.

QUESTION 10

How do you negotiate for a salary increase following the obtainment of a nonwork but work-related accomplishment like the completion of an M.B.A., C.P.A., etc.?

RESPONSES

A. Justify the going rate for your experience and ask for an increase based on those parameters.

B. Talk about career development, what you are capable of contributing, and what the company's needs are.

C. Understand BEFORE you begin work toward this non-work but work-related accomplishment how obtaining it will impact your salary or status within the company. Never assume anything.

D. Talk about it before you start the program. Find out what the company policy is. It is best to negotiate for a new title—the salary will follow.

G. The sad truth is to get any benefit for an M.B.A., C.P.A., etc., you will probably need to change jobs.

L. Discuss this issue prior to beginning any advanced degree or certificate program. It will set an anchor for future discussions and will help you to better understand your company's position. An advanced degree may have no significant impact on your compensation with your current employer. Knowing this early on will allow you to better utilize the educational and networking opportunities provided by the program.

Authors. It is a good idea to broach this subject when you begin as opposed to after you complete such an accomplishment. Together you can assess the extent to which such an accomplishment will add value. You can also talk about what changes in compensation might be warranted upon completion of the program to reflect this added value.

If you did not have this discussion before you completed the program, do not despair. It is still worth discussing. Explain in some detail how the organization can expect to benefit from the accomplishment. Ask them to reevaluate your current title and/or compensation in light of the enhanced benefit and value to them. If they resist, ask the employer to educate you regarding what criteria it would take to improve your compensation. Test the employer's willingness to create a contingency contract that more formally states that you will receive additional compensation upon completion of the criteria.

QUESTION 11

I was receiving tuition benefits for my M.B.A. when my company was acquired. How could I have renegotiated my position, perks, etc., following the corporate acquisition?

RESPONSES

B. In a big company, try to convince someone who has control of the issue to add a similar program. In a small company, try to get them to do a grandfather clause.

F. Turnover in these situations is often double that of normal times. We counsel our clients to actively recruit [in the case of an acquisition] their key players during the early stages of the new change. This should involve as great an effort as recruiting a new person to the firm. It is an excellent time for these valued employees to renegotiate their compensation packages.

G. Remember, when most companies acquire another, they usually try to adjust the benefits across the board to create an equal situation. Usually those from the company with the worst benefits come out best. In most cases, they bring the benefits up to the level of the highest good. This is usually the case, but not always. When new management comes in, they may not really want to have everyone from the old company. You may want to tread lightly until you have established yourself as a valuable asset.

I.   You can probably not renegotiate these issues unless the acquiring company has expected these costs as part of the acquisition. They do not know you and will, therefore, be less inclined to provide more until they do.

J.   It depends on a lot, including "who paid for the education." If you—rather than the company—footed the bill, you might have a good case. Go and see if the salary could be brought up to the correct standard that reflects the degree.

L.   Loss of such a benefit is a reality in many corporate consolidations. For the new company to offer this to you, they may have to incur the added cost of offering such a benefit to the tens, hundreds, or even thousands of existing employees. If they are unwilling to do so, you may be able to use mechanisms such as salary adjustments or bonuses to offset the differences.

Authors. We love the recommendations provided by the members of our expert panel. In fact, we suggest that you follow the advice outlined above. The only caveat is that we would approach the subject of the M.B.A. tuition now. If you do so, follow our recommends regarding question 10.

Stories from the Hiring Line

As we mentioned in our preface, experience is an invaluable commodity. The stories that follow will allow you to learn from the many experiences of our panel members. Each reflects a particularly positive, negative, or noteworthy experience. Each was an experience from which they learned a great deal and from which you can learn as well.

KNOW WHEN TO STOP

I had a candidate who renegotiated three times on salary expectations. He was submitted originally to our client at a salary of 50K. One week passed and just before the interview he told me he wanted 55K. Then on his application, he filled out that he needed 58K for a salary. Finally, after the offer was made at 58K, the candidate wanted 62K. He indicated that he had another offer at 62K.

Needless to say, the client did not match his salary of 62K because he could not produce the offer letter from the other company. The client even nearly rescinded the offer. After much damage control, the client had a change in heart.

Result: the candidate took the job at 58K. However, the client was very put out that he'd played games with them. Bottom line: Don't get carried away to the point where the client rescinds the offer.

Authors' Note. This is a good example of how a candidate can create his own unnecessary and potentially costly speed bumps.

This candidate made a number of mistakes you should avoid, including: discussing salary before the employer offered the job, bidding his salary bottom line instead of his target for fear that he would be dropped from the candidate pool, playing bait-and-switch in an attempt to correct his mistakes, misrepresenting his alternatives, requesting a salary amount he could not justify, and talking walk away when he would not. Given the number of errors made, he was lucky things turned out as well as they did.

BEWARE THE POLITICS

We were doing a search for a marketing director for one of our clients. The candidate who "won" the job had been with the same company for about ten years. This was the only company that this person had been with since college, and, therefore, he had never negotiated a job offer. Their offer was about a 20 percent raise in base salary, a higher bonus, plus the opportunity to take part in the IPO [initial public offering] of this prospective employer. After receiving the offer, the candidate called some of the other directors within the company to see what their bonuses were, along with other perks like mobile phones, car allowances, etc. The candidate then "counteroffered" with some of the things that he thought he should have. Unfortunately, these people had already called the VP of Human Resources, who then rescinded the offer. The VP of HR, along with the "hiring manager" and other VPs, decided that this was a "red flag" on the candidate's "judgment" and "maturity." The VP of HR and hiring manager felt like the candidate had gone behind their backs to try and get more (after he had made a good faith agreement), and that this might become a problem in the future with other scenarios. Fair or not, this candidate did not understand the politics/art of negotiating, and it was a hard-learned lesson.

Authors' Note. Similar to the first story, it makes clear the cost of changing your strategy midstream and the unfortunate tendency to do this when candidates have not prepared sufficiently before receiving the offer. Preparation is the key.

This story also points out the importance of direct, honest communication. Always treat the other party with respect. Do not use strategies *before* you get the job that you would not use *on* the job (for example, going around a contact person to get information without getting their permission to do so). The choices you make now say a lot about the choices you will make tomorrow and every day.

CHANGE THE TITLE NOT THE SALARY

I have one suggestion to think about when negotiating for a new job and the salary is not what you expected. This scenario happened at FedEx recently. A candidate received an offer that was not quite as high as he expected. He found out through a friend who was currently working there that he should try to be brought in at the next level of promotion, which would be senior analyst, rather than analyst. The moral of the story is, find out what each level of promotion is and what is required to achieve the next level. If you think you have already achieved that level, then ask to be brought in at that level.

160

Authors' Note. Before you trade off an issue or worse, compromise on an issue, ask questions regarding why the employer is unable or unwilling to honor it. The information you get may allow you to create a solution that unties his/her hands. This example points out a solution that often works when the salary/compensation offered is insufficient and when you have the skill set to justify a change in title or position. Remember, most employers are concerned about "fairness" as it relates to internal equity. Find every opportunity to increase the value to the employer for doing what you want, not the costs.

THE VALUE OF THE DEAL

Just three days ago a candidate successfully negotiated a $5,000 signing bonus that he intends to use as tuition reimbursement. Since the company does not provide tuition reimbursement until an employee is vested for a year in the company, we worked it as a signing bonus. It took three days, we lost a bit of sleep, but once it shook out, we had an ecstatic candidate and a very happy company. Good things do happen.

Authors' Note. Just because an employer cannot give you the specific issue you asked for does not mean he/she is not able or motivated to give you the value you ask for. Remember, you are really more concerned about the value you get from the deal, not the specific form of that deal. Be flexible in terms of the specifics of the deal but firm regarding the value of the deal. When the employer can't do what you ask, help him/her find alternative ways to fulfill your underlying interest and bring you the value you seek.

ONLY MAKE A THREAT IF IT IS A PROMISE

We had a number of people over the years who demanded more based on the fact that others were making more. A number of them didn't really want to leave, but they said they would leave and they ended up having to do so. Don't say it if you don't mean it. Other people's deals have nothing to do with your deal. To bring them up will only make the boss mad, since you shouldn't be telling what you make.

In one case, a guy liked his job until he found out that others were making more than he was. He was really happy with his job until then. He said he would leave if we did not meet his demands. We didn't and he left. The unfortunate thing is that he did not really want to go and we did not really want him to go. I guess you could call this a lose-lose situation.

Authors' Note. Provide an anchor (in terms of a similar offer) only when you can justify it with an account. The comparisons you select may not be those selected by the employer when making fairness judgments. Be realistic and honest with yourself as well as the employer. When asking for a salary increase and a change in compensation, remember the following important rules:

1. You only get to go to the well so many times. Pick your battles. You will lose credibility and have less chance of getting what you ask for if you ask too often.

2. Carefully determine your skill set, seniority, performance record, value to the organization, and alternatives before selecting comparison to others.

3. If possible, use a *value added* rather than *fairness* approach initially. Focus on the value you bring and what you will do to enhance the value of the organization in return for the cost incurred in doing what you ask. Create a contingency contract if necessary. This approach avoids the issue of "others" altogether.

4. If you must use "fairness talk," acknowledge that each case is unique. Instead of comparing yourself to another individual, compare the value you bring (your input) versus your compensation level (your outcome) to the norms associated with the internal market as a whole or the external market.

5. Bring in the issue of alternative offers as information that supports your assertions regarding your value rather than as threat. In fact, do not bring up the possibility of a move until you are prepared to do so.

6. Do not attempt to renegotiate your compensation with your current employer if you have no intention of staying. Treat people with respect before, during, and after your employment with their organization. Burned bridges are really tough to cross.

IF YOU CAN AFFORD TO WALK AWAY

When I interviewed at my current firm (in my last semester of graduate school), they expressed that they were impressed with me and wanted me to come to work for them. What they had in mind was a trial period as an internship during my last few months of school, and we would just see how it went before agreeing to a full-time offer. I was not comfortable with this, as it would essentially limit my other opportunities. For one thing, I currently had another internship where I was also interviewing for a full-time job. By leaving that firm to work for this one, I would certainly burn that bridge. I really wanted to accept this offer but was not willing to do so by sacrificing my security and other options without a firm commitment. I told them I understood their reasons for wanting a trial run, but I would only agree to quit the first internship and work part time during the school year if I had an offer of full-time employment following graduation. By holding firm to this position and being willing to walk away from the offer, they finally agreed and made me a generous offer of full-time employment. (Luckily, it's been a successful choice on both parts.)

Authors' Note. If an impasse appears imminent due to the incompatibility of your interests (as was the case here) despite every attempt to align them, it is time to decide whether you can live with the offer. If what they offer exceeds both your bottom line and best alternative, accept the position. If it does not, carefully explain what it would take to have you accept an offer and why the current offer doesn't work for you. Then leave it to them to decide whether it's in their best interest to change the offer or let you go. Either way, don't make it personal. Exit the process with the same level of professionalism and grace you displayed when you entered.

- In response to these applicant questions, there are different ways to create and claim value effectively. Pick the one that's right for you.

- These actual scenarios can help you see what to do, what not to do, and when to take the offer and run with it!

10 FINAL THOUGHTS

They met again at her favorite restaurant.

"Chris, you look great!" said Sara. "That new suit brings out the blue in your eyes and you are absolutely beaming. Does this mean what I think it means?"

"Why don't I fill you in over a bottle of champagne," Chris told her with a wink. "For the first time in our lives, we can afford it."

We have come to the end of this book but the beginning of your job-related negotiations. By now you should have a comprehensive model for thinking about and approaching your negotiation. You should also have a working knowledge of the tactics that you will need to succeed. Congratulations and the best of luck (although you will not need it given what you know now). Before you begin, we leave you with a few final thoughts, including the most important points to remember and a list of do's and don'ts.

To help you remember, we have enclosed a summary card of this information for your review. After you read this section, close the book and get going!

Top Ten Things to Do

NEGOTIATE

There are few costs and many benefits to negotiating an offer. Remember that those who negotiate are likely to make several million more over a lifetime than those who accept an offer without negotiating. Consequently, the question is not "if" you should negotiate, but "how" you should negotiate. This book answers the how question by teaching you a constructive, professional, value-added approach to negotiation.

DO YOUR HOMEWORK

Nothing helps negotiation more than good preparation. Get as much information as possible about the current job market and your value in it. Use every resource available to you, including your network of family, friends, and coworkers, university placement centers, the library, and the Internet, as outlined in chapter 2. The more you know, the more you will be able to accurately set your expectations and explain your worth.

Create a preference sheet. A preference sheet will force you to determine what you want, why you want it, and how much you want it. It will also help you compare one offer to another, propose counteroffers, and track movement on the part of the employer. Your preference sheet should include all of the issues of relevance to you, issue ranges, issue weights, underlying interests, and package range (including your target and bottom line).

Identify your alternatives. Having more than one offer will enhance your negotiating power and help you to negotiate a more attractive offer for two reasons: First, it will decrease your tendency to think that you need the job more than the job needs you. Second, it will enhance the employer's confidence in you and perception of your worth, confirming his/her wise decision to hire you.

Order Your Interviews

Early interviews provide a good opportunity to practice your technique, so schedule low-priority interviews very early on. These practice sessions should be immediately followed by your highest priority interviews so that you can avoid the dilemma associated with an early exploding offer. If you are unable to avoid one of these bombs despite your best efforts, duck and run for cover, as instructed in chapter 7.

Enlist the Other Side's Assistance

Negotiation does not need to be an adversarial process. Break the ice with your prospective employer by thanking them for considering you. Create some professional investment on their side by highlighting the *unique* value that you bring to the job. Remember, you want them to be committed to hiring you before they even know what it will cost them. You can do a lot to enlist the other side's assistance in this negotiation by finding a personal connection. If you can find a personal connection to the other side, they will see you as someone they can trust and someone they would like to hire. Maximize your overall value by maintaining goodwill, even with employers whose offers you reject.

RESPOND TO AN OFFER WITH QUESTIONS

The best response to an offer is a question. Use your questions to educate yourself about the employer's preferences and limitations by asking who, why, why not, when, and how. Countering an offer before such questions are answered is like shooting an arrow without a clear target. Wasted arrows are difficult to retrieve, so use questions to help you aim before you fire. You can also use questions to help signal your interest in issues that are not yet on the table.

PREPARE YOUR COUNTEROFFER CAREFULLY

Your counteroffer provides an important opportunity to anchor the employer, so lead with your target. Be sure to justify your counteroffer with an account that both explains and supports the validity of your request. Use "gain-language" to frame the employer and increase his/her commitment to an agreement. Create contingencies that align your interests with those of the employer and reduce their risk by ensuring him/her a return on the requested investment in you.

EXPAND THE PIE IN ORDER TO CLAIM VALUE

When you expand the pie, you make it easier to claim more value for yourself, and you make it easier to give the other side enough value for them to say "Yes!" to what you want. Often we are so sure that a negotiation is going to be a "tug-of-war" that we fail to recognize opportunities to expand the pie. Be on the lookout for compatible issues and opportunities to make trade-offs that help both sides, or help one side at no cost to the other. Adding and fractioning issues often provide important opportunities to expand the pie. Proposing multiple packages can also help you identify settlement options that do more to satisfy both sides' interests.

KEEP YOUR EYES ON THE PRIZE

Your goal should be to obtain an attractive salary and compensation package while improving your relationship with your future employer. This is not only possible, it is probable if you use the techniques we have outlined in this book. Always maintain your commitment to obtaining your underlying interests but remain flexible as to "how" you obtain them.

GET IT IN WRITING

Experience has taught us that most people are honorable and well-intentioned. While most verbal offers are likely to be honored, there's no harm in requesting your offer in writing. Having done so, be sure to review the written offer carefully before accepting it.

KNOW WHEN TO WALK AWAY

It is important to recognize when to just say no in a negotiation. Try to make the prospective employer play their last card before you walk away. If you do decide to walk away, always take care to exit the interview and negotiation process as constructively and professionally as you entered it. As one author's dad used to advise, "It never pays to burn your bridges." The interview process provides a marvelous opportunity to network with people who you might run into again in your career.

Top Ten Things "Not to Do"

DON'T NEGOTIATE PREMATURELY

Try to avoid discussions regarding your salary and compensation goals until after you have been offered the job. Also avoid responding to an offer until after you have analyzed the offer and asked pointed questions.

DON'T PLAY THE GAME IN THE EMPLOYER'S NEIGHBORHOOD

There is a lot of uncertainty in most salary and compensation negotiations. Don't let the employer use your uncertainty as a weapon against you in your negotiation. Do your homework so that you will understand what to expect, rather than being anchored by the employer's offers or accounts. Whenever possible, get the game played in *your* neighborhood by using anchors and accounts and by framing your offers as gains for the other side.

Don't Tell the Employer Your Bottom Line Unless You Are Ready to Walk

Sharing your bottom line will change the discussion from a negotiation to a transaction (take-it-or-leave-it) situation. Employers are likely to respond with an offer that just exceeds the bottom line, so be careful what you wish for. This also means the anchors you use in negotiation should always be your targets—not ranges.

Don't Compromise

Good negotiators understand the importance of expanding the pie. A compromise does not help expand the pie because a compromise does not take advantage of the different value negotiators attach to issues. When you compromise, you often miss an important opportunity to expand the pie and that means leaving money on the table.

Don't Make Unilateral Concessions

Negotiation is a process of give and take. In fact, good negotiators can often increase the value of an agreement to themselves even while giving something up to the other side. This *never* happens, however, when you make unilateral concessions. If you are going to make a concession, you should always try to make the concession in exchange for a concession from the other side on an issue of greater value to you. Packaging issues together provides an opportunity for you to give the other side more of what they want while getting more of what you want at the same time.

DON'T LET YOUR EMOTIONS TAKE OVER

Emotions are potential value killers. Try to remember that the employer is not the problem. The issues to be negotiated are the problem. If you or the employer start to get emotional, ask for some additional time to consider the offer and agree on a convenient time to reconvene.

DON'T MISREPRESENT

A good reputation takes a lifetime to build and a mere moment to destroy. Consider how you want to be perceived and remembered at the end of your career. Comport yourself accordingly now.

DON'T BE A VICTIM OF THE WINNER'S CURSE OR THE LOSER'S CURSE

Preparation is critical to maintaining your perspective during a negotiation, and maintaining your perspective is the key to a successful negotiation. Carefully determine the issues that are important to you and why you want them. Remain flexible and realistic. Keeping your eye on the prize will increase the probability of recognizing and obtaining it when it is offered.

DON'T RESORT (OR REACT) TO FAIRNESS LANGUAGE

Fair is one of the four-letter "F" words in negotiation. Rather than talking about what is fair—which often brings emotions into the mix—use justified anchoring, contingency contracts, and other techniques to keep an employer's eyes focused on the prize. Use the negotiation to educate your employer about how much return—how much value—he/she can expect from investing in you.

DON'T TALK "WALK AWAY" UNTIL YOU MEAN IT

Threatening to walk away—to end the negotiation—can be powerful but dangerous. Walking away means depriving the other side of any value you bring to the table. Unfortunately, it also means depriving you of any value they bring to the table. You should only walk away when you have exhausted *all* the avenues we have explored in this book for expanding the pie and claiming value. You should only threaten to walk away when your threat is a promise.

Things to Remember

YOUR GOAL IS THE COMPENSATION PACKAGE THAT OFFERS YOU THE MOST VALUE

After reading this book, this should be obvious. But it bears repeating, as do a couple of other points it implies.

DON'T GET FIXATED ON ANY SINGLE ISSUE

In particular, remember that this is *not* a "salary" negotiation. This is a negotiation about *everything* that comes with accepting a job. When you add up the value that an offer provides you, don't forget about: the company's prospects and your opportunities for promotion, the cost of living, your lifestyle in the city where you'd work, and the quality of your coworkers.

One of the other intangibles you will be negotiating is goodwill concerning your relationship with the employers. It is critical that you maintain a calm and professional tone throughout *all* of your negotiations. Do not let any disagreements become personal. In the negotiation, employers are unlikely to help applicants they have come to dislike. Worse yet, you don't want to get things started on the wrong foot with the employer whose offer you do accept.

Even if you have to talk "walk away" to get what you want, do it in a calm, professional, and even friendly manner. You may want a job from that employer in the future, so you'll want a favorable impression of you to be the first impression they think of next time.

Remember, your goal in this negotiation is to get the best package you can—but not "at any cost." These costs—including your reputation among employers—are also part of the overall value you negotiate.

WE EXPAND THE PIE TO CLAIM VALUE

Everyone seems to understand that negotiation is about claiming as much as you can for yourself. What is new for most novice negotiators is the idea of expanding the pie. The more value you find, the more you can claim for yourself. The more value you find, the more you can give the other side.

Negotiation is not about expanding the pie. **Negotiation is about claiming value.** Expanding the pie can help you claim value, but it isn't always *necessary,* and it isn't ever *sufficient.* Even when you can expand the pie, you still may have to work hard to claim your share.

WHAT IF THEY WON'T PLAY?

Negotiation training can be a real eye-opening experience for many novice negotiators. Having read this book, we hope you are cured of the illusion that negotiation is about dividing up a fixed pie, or that negotiation is about "beating" the other side.

Negotiation is about meeting your goals. If the world isn't a fixed pie, you can meet your goals and still help your employers meet theirs as well. Applicants and employers *don't value all issues the same,* so there are always opportunities to expand the pie. And that means there are always opportunities to help both sides achieve their goals.

But what if the employer doesn't know this? What if the employer thinks the world is a fixed pie? What if the employer thinks negotiation is a tug-of-war? You need to know the employer's interests to find all the value that is available. If the employers think the idea is to beat you, you have to give them enough or frame them enough so that the employers think they did.

If you've done your homework and if you ask a lot of questions, using everything you have learned in this book, you can do that. It may be difficult and it may take time—but you can do it. And every time you do, the next time will be that much easier.

So Now Just Go Out and Do It!

ENDNOTES

On page xi, our U.S. Department of Labor statistics come from the department's monthly Employment & Earnings publication, Volume 46, Number 7, 1999, in which they report statistics regarding the unemployment rate adjusted by season and causality.

On page 6, the study comparing the outcomes of men and women negotiating job offers was conducted by B. Gerhart and S. Rynes and is titled "Determinants and Consequences of Salary Negotiations by Male and Female MBA Graduates" (*Journal of Applied Psychology*, Volume 76, 1991, pp. 256–262).

On page 40, the speed with which first impressions are made in interviews is discussed in R. D. Arvey and J. E. Campion's "The Employment Interview: A Summary and Review of Recent Research," in G. F. Dreher and P. R. Sackett (eds.), *Perspectives on Employee Staffing and Selection,* (1983, pp. 289–318, Homewood, Illinois: R. D. Irwin, Inc.)

On page 58, this concept of being tough on the issues but gentle on the people first gained prominence following the publication of Fisher and Ury's *Getting to Yes: Negotiating Agreement Without Giving In,* (1981, Houghton, Mifflin & Company).

On page 64, some of Mary Parker Follet's best writings are presented in *Dynamic Administration: The Collected Papers of Mary Parker Follet*, eds. E. M. Fox and L. Urwick (New York: Hippocrene, 1982).

On page 65, the notion of compatible issues is discussed by L. Thompson in "Information Exchange in Negotiation" (*Journal of Experimental Social Psychology*, Volume 27, 1991, pp. 161–179).

On page 87, we describe the excellent strategy conceived by Robert Robinson for responding to exploding offers. The details of this strategy are discussed in his article "Defusing the Exploding Offer: The Farpoint Gambit" (*Negotiation Journal*, 1995, pp. 277–85).

On page 90, the notion of framing is discussed in detail by A. Tversky and D. Kahneman in "The Framing of Decisions and the Psychology of Choice" (*Science*, Volume 211, 1981, pp. 453–58).

On page 92, the use of accounts to manage attributions is raised by R. Bies in "The Predicament of Injustice: The Management of Moral Outrage," in B. M. Staw and L. L. Cummings (eds.), *Research in Organizational Behavior*, Volume 9, 1987, pp. 289–319 (Greenwich, Connecticut: JAI Press).

On page 104, M. Bazerman discusses the "winner's curse" and other negotiation biases in "Why Negotiations Go Wrong," in *Psychology Today*, June 1986, pp. 54–58.

On page 108, the traditional notion of fairness is captured by J. S. Adams in "Toward an Understanding of Inequity" (*Journal of Abnormal and Social Psychology*, Volume 67, 1963, pp. 422–36).

ABOUT THE AUTHORS

Dr. Robin L. Pinkley is Chairman of the Organizational Behavior Business Policy Department and Director of the American Airlines Center for Labor-Relations and Conflict Resolution at the Edwin L. Cox School of Business at Southern Methodist University.

Dr. Pinkley's research focuses on sources and consequences of negotiator power and the strategic application of "value context theory." This research has earned Dr. Pinkley the Edwin L. Cox 1994 Outstanding Researcher Award, a Corrigan Fellowship, a Dorothy Cullum Fellowship, and a Marilyn & Leo F. Corrigan Junior Faculty Endowment. She also received Southern Methodist University's Golden Mustang Award for her innovative teaching.

Dr. Pinkley was an associate editor of the *International Journal of Conflict Management* and is a frequent speaker in management development programs as well as a negotiation consultant for corporate and government organizations. Clients include ARCO, General Electric, Kodak, Mobil, Computerland, Banc-Tec, NASA, Lockheed Martin, Southwestern Bell Company,

AMRESCO, Remington Hotel Corporation, and SBC Communications, Inc.

Dr. Pinkley has been interviewed on CNN, ABC, CBS, NBC, and FOX as well as quoted in newspapers and magazines such as the *Wall Street Journal, New York Times, Chicago Tribune, Dallas Morning News, Los Angeles Times, USA Today, Money, Fortune, Redbook,* and *The Ladies Home Journal.*

She lives in Dallas, Texas.

Gregory B. Northcraft is the Harry J. Gray Professor of Executive Leadership in the Department of Business Administration and Labor and Industrial Relations, at the University of Illinois.

His major research interests include negotiation and conflict management, collaboration in teams, managerial decision making, and employee motivation and job design, particularly in high-technology manufacturing settings. He has authored or coauthored articles and invited chapters appearing in such places as *Organizational Behavior and Human Decision Processes, Academy of Management Journal, Academy of Management Review, Journal of Applied Psychology, Decision Sciences,* and *Organization Science.*

Professor Northcraft has done consulting and management training worldwide for a variety of manufacturing and service sector firms. He is coauthor of the text *Organizational Behavior: A Management Challenge* and is currently editor of the *Academy of Management Journal.*

He lives in Champaign-Urbana, Illinois.

INDEX

INDEX